THE KEY TO ART

THE KEY TO MODERN ART
OF THE EARLY 20TH CENTURY

A Bateman/Search Press Pocket Guide

Lourdes Cirlot
Professor of Art History

Search Press, Tunbridge Wells, England
in association with
David Bateman, Auckland, New Zealand

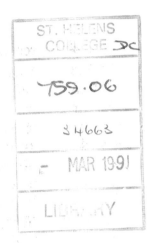
Words that appear in **bold** type are listed in the glossary.

First published in Great Britain 1990
Search Press Limited
Wellwood, North Farm Road
Tunbridge Wells, Kent, TN2 3DR

In association with David Bateman Ltd.
32-34 View Road, Glenfield, Auckland, New Zealand

ISBN 0 85532 664 6

A David Bateman Book

Printed in Spain

INTRODUCTION

MARC CHAGALL. *I and the Village*. 1911. Museum of Modern Art, New York.
This is one of Chagall's first paintings after he settled in Paris. It shows his nostalgia for the small Russian villages of his youth and his deep interest in the country life with which he was so familiar. The whole atmosphere, the setting in which both people and animals are depicted, is reminiscent of the German Expressionist school in Munich.

General Appreciation

Faced with the vastly differing trends and styles of 20th century art, it is almost impossible to approach an appreciation of it in the same way that we do for other periods. In general, most art historians accept the established terminology of styles, many described by words ending in "-ism." Following this classification, this book will deal with painting, sculpture, and architecture as expressions of a particular art style or "-ism" rather than as separate subjects.

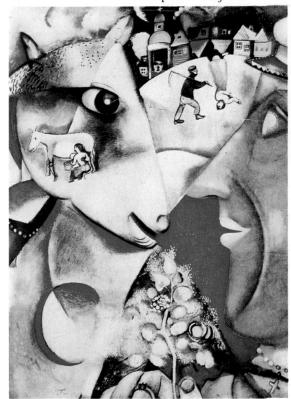

We will start by establishing two well-defined groups: those with early modern tendencies and those which appeared after the Second World War. We are dealing with two groups which, though different, share certain similarities, especially the dependency of the post-war groups upon the earlier ones. But the final result—the art object itself—is totally distinct in each group. Perhaps the most relevant characteristic of this century's art in comparison with that of other periods is its break from all past art. From the beginning of the 20th century, art broke loose from everything that had already been established. Art historians agree, however, that it was during the second half of the 19th century that the first radical changes occurred in artistic awareness, and these changes can be said to be the beginnings of this separation. The year 1863, in which Manet painted his *Déjeuner sur l'Herbe (Luncheon on the Grass)*, is considered to mark the start of the chronology of contemporary painting. It is the boldness exhibited in this painting, as well as the formal aspects, that allow critics to discern the pattern of things to come.

The majority of early modern artists were clearly influenced by Impressionism during their student days and by Post-Impressionism later in their careers. Looking at paintings from the beginning of the century, we can appreciate how Cézanne and Van Gogh influenced the modern artists, who were all working in their different styles or "-isms." For example, Van Gogh's use of thick coats of paint and curved lines were among the first of man' daring achievements. His range of intense ? exciting colour, found also in the works of Gau led many artists to set new goals in their experiments with colour.

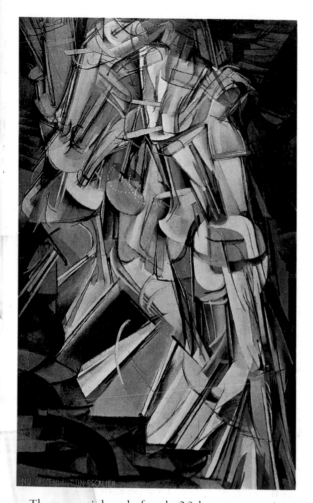

MARCEL DUCHAMP.
*Nude Descending a
Staircase, No. 2. 1912.*
**Museum of Art,
Philadelphia.**
Duchamp's contacts with
Cubism and **Futurism** are
evident in this picture.
The effect of movement
was created by the Futurists
through the use of a
technique called simul-
taneity. Duchamp has used
small half-circles, made up
of tiny white dots, to give
the impression of turning
movements.

The essential goal of early 20th century artists
was to bring an experimental atmosphere to the
artistic world. Painters and sculptors avoided
imitation, and as we shall see, took refuge in in-
creasingly daring experiments with materials,
techniques, and arrangements. We have only to
look at **Cubism,** one of the most important 20th
century styles, to see the extent of these experimental concepts. **Collage,** a technique introduced
by the Cubists, played an important role for many
modern artists.

Scientific achievements of the early 20th century influenced not only industrial progress but also contemporary art. Other factors also influenced these new styles. Philosophers indirectly helped shape new concepts in art with their probings about the nature of space and time. **German Expressionism, Fauvism,** Cubism, and

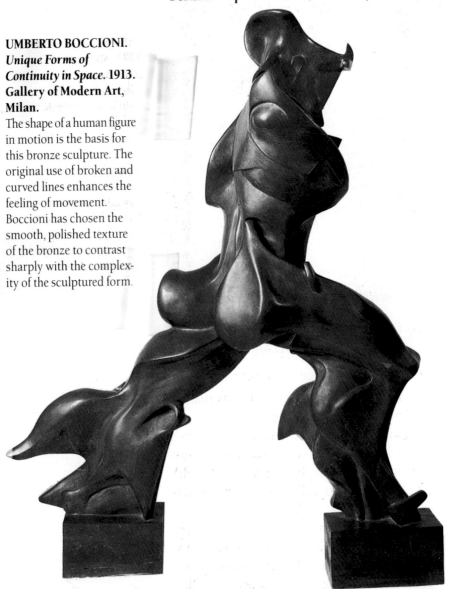

UMBERTO BOCCIONI.
Unique Forms of Continuity in Space. **1913. Gallery of Modern Art, Milan.**
The shape of a human figure in motion is the basis for this bronze sculpture. The original use of broken and curved lines enhances the feeling of movement. Boccioni has chosen the smooth, polished texture of the bronze to contrast sharply with the complexity of the sculptured form.

Futurism are all movements that were influenced by scientists and philosophers.

Modernism, a concept derived from the primary philosophy at the beginning of this century, is a key part of these early styles. To be modern implied innovation and change, and thus a rejec-

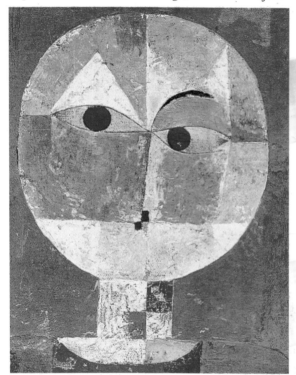

PAUL KLEE. *Senecio*. 1922. Museum of Fine Arts, Basel.
Klee's individuality makes it difficult to include him in any of the different artistic styles that he used. His fluctuation between **figurative** and **abstract** art is one of the main characteristics of his work. This well-known Swiss artist was a member of *Der blaue Reiter* and the **Bauhaus School.**

tion of the past. Architects, sculptors, painters, and designers all sought new solutions that reflected the modern world. Machines were seen as having an almost magical quality from which many artistic achievements originated. It must not be forgotten, though, that the early styles were conceived in a peculiar atmosphere—that of the First World War. Different schools brought different attitudes to the same topics. To the Futurists, the machine was a symbol of the modernity they desired. To the Dadaists, it was a symbol of the progress which led to conflict.

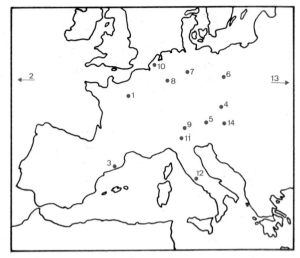

JOAN MIRÓ. *Dutch Interior.* 1928. Museum of Modern Art, New York.
By the end of the 1920s, Miró's style was completely formed and at its peak in a work such as this. Miró uses all sorts of signs as elements in his paintings, all treated in his own characteristic way. The relationship of human figures, animals, vegetables, celestial bodies, and other constructions is very surrealistic. The bright colours that he used give his work a great sense of joy.

Geography and Chronology

The abundance of different styles, or "-isms," is one characteristic of the 20th century art world. Another important characteristic is the constant interplay among the different, but coexisting, currents in Europe and North America.

Modernism ruled artistic horizons at the end of the 19th century and into the 20th century. The year 1905 is seen as the starting date for the many new tendencies which together make up the early modern style.

Fauvism first appeared in Paris in 1905, the same year in which the **Die Brücke** (The Bridge) group first manifested the start of the complex German Expressionist movement in Dresden.

In 1907, Cubism appeared in the Paris school. It soon gained converts across Europe, but their work did not always follow an orthodox path.

Italian Futurism made its appearance in 1907. It is formally connected with the earlier movements, though its ideologies may differ. In Russia, a mix of Futurist and Cubist elements produced what is known as **Rayonism,** Russia's contribution to avant-garde art of the time.

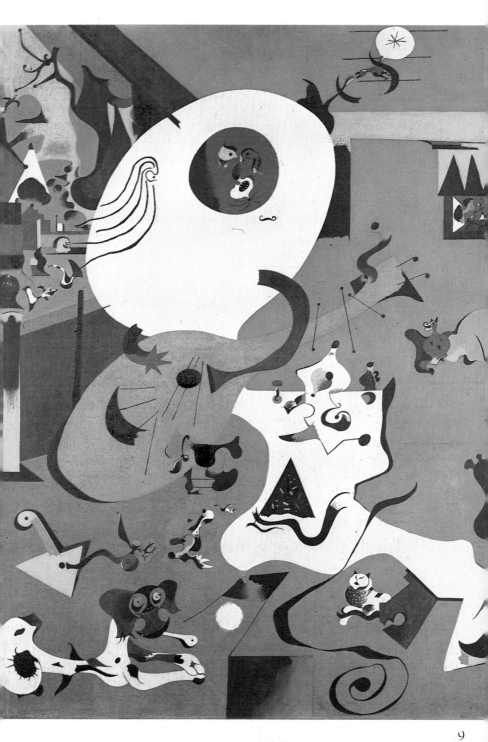

In 1911, after all the innovations of the Dresden Expressionists had reached a peak, a second type of Expressionism was born in Munich. The group, known as *Der blaue Reiter* (The Blue Rider) was directed by Vasily Kandinsky. Of equal importance with their artistic achievements are their contributions to the theory of art.

The outbreak of the First World War created a vacuum in the art world. But 1914 saw the rise, in Russia, of **Suprematism**. This school opened new horizons for **Abstractionism,** which was started four years earlier by Kandinsky. Suprematist concepts are closest, in their strongly geometric style, to the Dutch group called **De Stijl,** which appeared in 1917. The previous year, **Dadaism** had sprung up in Zurich, quickly spreading to Berlin, Hanover, and Cologne by 1918. Artists and writers in Paris and New York accepted Dadaism, and later **Surrealism,** making these truly international movements. The year 1924 marked the beginning of the Surrealist movement with the publication of the first Surrealist manifesto by the intellectual leader of the group, André Breton. Surrealism attracted many followers, including several artists who emigrated to the United States before and during the Second World War. They profoundly influenced North American art.

Parallel to Dadaism and Surrealism, which attempted to express the irrational, there were other movements which had total rationality as their basis.

In Germany, the Bauhaus School was founded at Weimar in 1919, influencing art in many media. In architecture, the Chicago School can be considered one of the precursors of the Bauhaus. Adolf Loos, from Vienna, was the founder of **Functionalism,** which ruled architectural thought for the first half of the century.

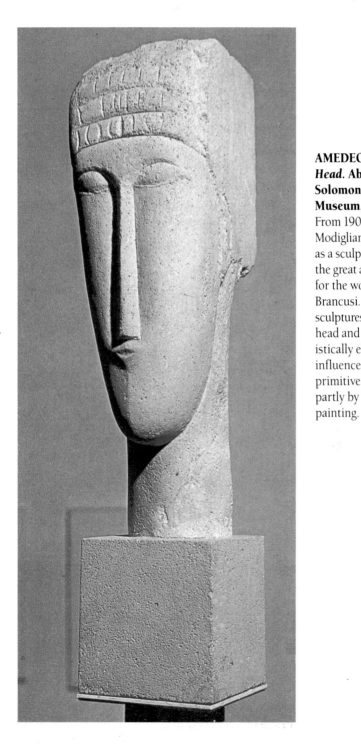

AMEDEO MODIGLIANI.
Head. **About 1911.**
Solomon R. Guggenheim
Museum, New York.
From 1909 to 1914,
Modigliani worked chiefly
as a sculptor, due in part to
the great admiration he felt
for the work of Constantin
Brancusi. Most of his
sculptures are of the human
head and are character-
istically elongated,
influenced partly by
primitive sculptures and
partly by Italian Mannerist
painting.

In the 1920s, Germany was a melting pot of ideas. Alongside the Bauhaus and Dada movements were many other artists, grouped together as *Neue Sachlichkeit* (New Realism). They made use of elements chosen from early Expressionism and pushed them to their very limits.

The Artist and Contemporary Society

With the increased interest in collecting art at the end of the 19th century, a new character appeared on the scene—the art dealer. The art dealer's task was to make contact between the buyer and the artist. Apart from spotting new talent, art dealers had to have a thorough knowledge of the whole range of art. They had to be able to distinguish the good from the bad. Art dealers also had to know the tastes of their clients and be able to offer them the right works for their collections at the right time.

The art dealer had become such an important figure by the beginning of this century that few artists could sell their works without contracting with a dealer.

Later, some dealers opened their own galleries in major cities to exhibit the work of their protegés. It became clear that a work of art was just another object to be traded, like stocks and bonds. Prices of art works fluctuated just as prices fluctuate on the stock exchange, and often for reasons just as inexplicable.

Today, many different types of contracts are arranged between artists and galleries, and the art world has a well-established trading system.

PABLO PICASSO.
Portrait of Gertrude Stein.
1906. Metropolitan Museum of Art, New York.
Picasso here shows us more than the mere physical likeness of his subject. He has caught something of the psychology of Gertrude Stein, whose later writings describing Picasso's work are very important to art historians. His treatment of her eyes makes them perhaps the most expressive part of the face. The slight asymmetry he used anticipates changes still to come in the art world. The geometry of the whole face, however, expresses the rigidity of pre-Cubist work of the time.

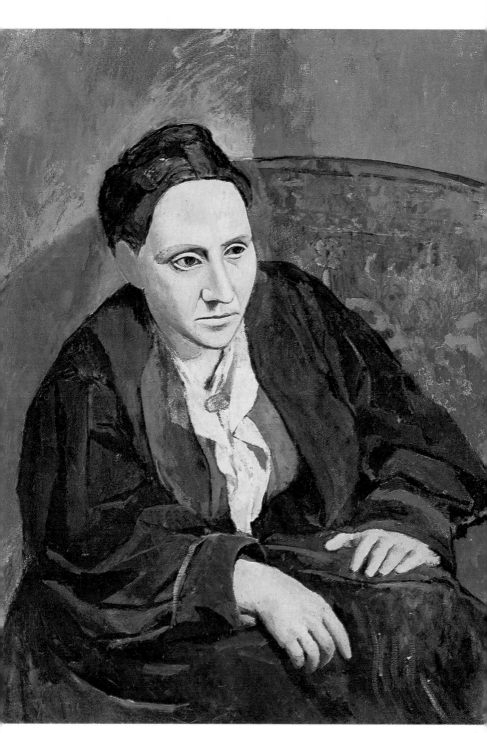

13

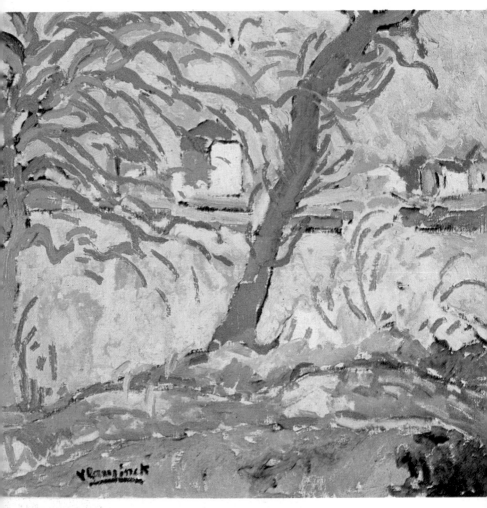

MAURICE DE VLAMINCK. *The Banks of the Seine at Carrières-sur-Seine.* **1906. Private Collection.** The influence of Van Gogh is immediately evident in this canvas, with the curved lines Vlaminck used to portray his subject. Fauvist landscapes, particularly those of Vlaminck, contain characteristically recognizable tree forms, which became almost a trademark of the movement.

THE –ISMS

Fauvism

We owe the concept of Fauvism to an art critic named Louis Vauxcelles. In 1905, he attended the Autumn Salon in Paris, where he found a series of richly, almost overpoweringly, coloured paintings displayed side by side with a small classical-style statue. The contrast between the two was so striking that he is said to have exclaimed, *"Donatello parmi les fauves"* (a Donatello amongst the wild beasts). From that moment, the group of artists, of which Matisse

HENRI MATISSE.
Portrait with Green Stripe. **1905.**
Museum of Fine Arts, Copenhagen.
A head and shoulders portrait of the artist's wife is the centrepiece of this composition. The most interesting aspect of the picture is that Matisse has not copied the physical features of his wife, but has given us his own interpretation of her face. Colour is everything in this picture. To use a green stripe, complementing the reds which predominate in the portrait, as a representation of the subject's nose, shows considerable audacity.

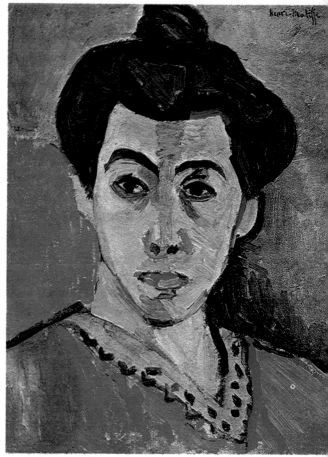

15

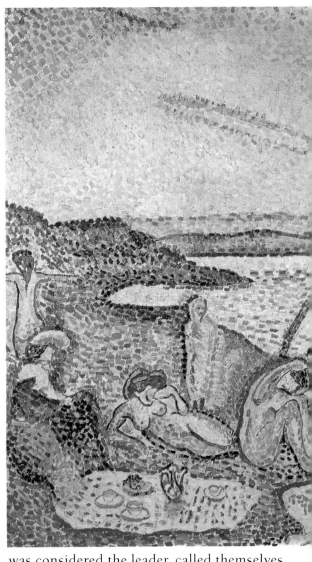

was considered the leader, called themselves Fauves (Wild Beasts).

Though Fauvism has long been considered the first avant-garde style to break with traditional techniques of painting, it should be remembered that Fauvism itself is a synthesis, a grouping together of different and often incongruous or inharmonious elements.

Within Fauvism, it is not difficult to trace elements which belong to earlier styles of the previous

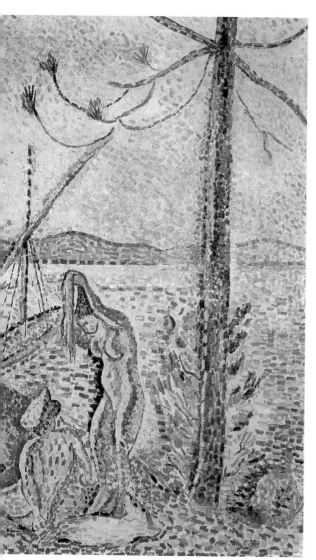

HENRI MATISSE. *Luxe, Calme, et Volupté.* **1904-05. Private Collection.**

This is the first in a series of paintings dedicated to the theme of "Luxury, Calm and Sensuality" from a poem by Baudelaire, a 19th century French poet. Though Matisse has used his **divisionist** technique in this painting, the geometrical accuracy he followed when distributing the colours on the canvas is a prelude to the Fauvist conception of painting. The range of colours used overrides the formal composition of the painting. It is this use of complementary colour that typifies the contrasts of the Fauvists.

century—Impressionism, Post-Impressionism, and Symbolism.

To understand how works from these schools influenced Henri Matisse, André Derain, Maurice de Vlaminck, Raoul Dufy, and Kees van Dongen, the principal Fauves, it must be remembered that when they were still studying art, the works of the earlier artists were being recognized and acclaimed by Paris society. Matisse, the oldest of the Fauves, had studied at the Ecole des Beaux

Arts in Paris with the Symbolist painter Gustave Moreau. Moreau favoured a revolutionary teaching method, very different from those used in most art academies of his day. He wanted to discourage students from merely copying the style of painters whose works they studied in the Louvre, but he wanted them to retain the essential elements of the masters and to use these in their own compo-

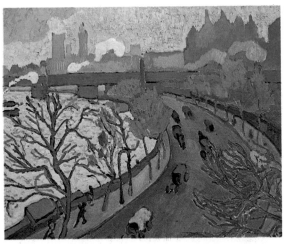

ANDRÉ DERAIN.
Westminster Bridge.
1905. The Louvre, Paris.
Undoubtedly influenced by the series of pictures which Claude Monet had painted in London, Derain chose several well-known views of the city for his subjects in 1905. Here we can compare the plain, mono-chrome architectural forms to the bridge, the river, and the trees, where contrasts of colour reign supreme The tree forms are typical of the Fauvists.

sitions. Moreau's opposition to "copying" became one of the most important principles of Fauvism. In any Fauvist painting, no representation of reality can be seen. In this, Fauvism differs from the Impressionist and Post-Impressionist schools, but it retains a similarity in the painting techniques used.

Some early works of the Fauvist school demonstrate a **divisionist technique,** as well as the use of thick coats of paint. Matisse and Derain, however, gradually abandoned divisionism, choosing a freer style and more vigorous brushwork. This technique, together with a new concept of colour, is one of the more formal characteristics of Fauvism.

The most important achievement of Fauvist painters was the clear independence of colour and form. Colour became the main element of a painting. It was even more important than the subject.

Despite their very advanced ideas on colour, Matisse and the Fauvists still painted subjects that had attracted artists at the end of the previous century. Country scenes and views of cities, portraits, interiors, and still lifes were still favourites.

Another characteristic of Fauvist artists is their interest in natural light. Matisse and Derain experimented with chromatic changes in Collioure during the summer of 1905. These changes were made possible by the bright, intense sunlight they found there. Shaded areas contrast with the more attractive coloured zones in their work, but nowhere are there sombre dark patches.

Fauvism gives colour a new vitality and dynamism. Light brushwork and dabs of paint are less important than the sheer exuberance of the colours used.

German Expressionism

The Expressionist movement developed mainly in Germany, and it was clearly rooted in 19th century Romanticism. Its revolutionary character, particularly in its later stages, makes it easy to

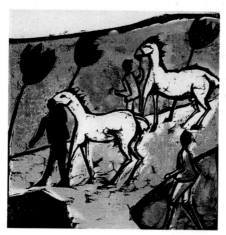

ERICK HECKEL. *White Horses*. 1912. Sprengel Museum, Hanover.
This is one of Heckel's many works in which he uses the technique of woodcut. It was a very popular technique, used not only by the Dresden artists, but by most German Expressionists. As an art form, its roots in Germany go back to the Middle Ages. Therefore, it is not surprising that a group of 20th century artists, who felt strongly attracted to that period, should decide to revive the traditional style.

distinguish from other art trends. Expressionism was more than an art style or a musical or literary trend. It was a way of experiencing the world.

KARL SCHMIDT-ROTTLUFF. *Dangast Countryside.* 1910. Stedelijk Museum, Amsterdam.

All the painters of the *Die Brücke* school tried to paint landscapes. They rejected traditional methods and used their own distinctive style instead. Tortured, zigzag lines produce compositions full of despair and anguish. The use of intense and contrasting colours also adds to the aggressiveness of their paintings.

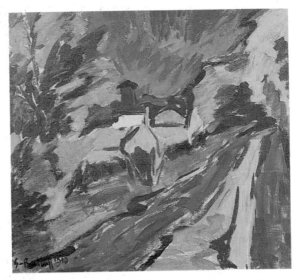

ERNST LUDWIG KIRCHNER. *Five Women in the Street.* 1913. Wallraf-Richartz Museum, Cologne.

The series of paintings in which Kirchner used the street as a theme are among some of the most interesting by this *Die Brücke* artist. The subjects, always in their best clothes, are treated ironically. Faces, clothes, and attitudes portray a carefree and uncaring middle class, totally unaware of the problems that would soon lead to the disaster of the First World War.

The aestheticism of the Expressionists reflects the social conditions leading up to the start of the First World War. Anguish, terror, misery, and oppression are frequent subjects for Expressionist paintings, prints, and sculptures, and many conceal a cry of fear.

The beginning of the Expressionist movement can be attributed to the formation, in 1905, of the *Die Brücke* group in Dresden, Germany. This group was founded by Ernst Ludwig Kirchner, Erich Heckel, Friedrich Bleyl, and Karl Schmidt-Rottluff, who were all architecture students. The celebrated Emil Nolde joined the group in 1906, but he only worked with them for a couple of months.

All the artists in the Dresden group were accomplished woodcarvers, in the best German tradition. It is in their woodcuts that the connections with Freudian psychoanalysis are best seen. In Vienna, during the early part of the century, Sigmund Freud was disrupting the cultural scene with his theories about sexuality. Naturally, his influence was great in German-speaking countries. It is not surprising, therefore, that

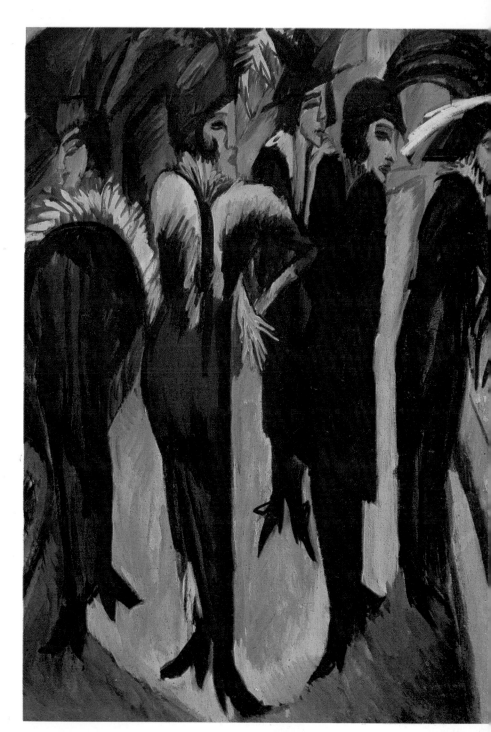

VASILY KANDINSKY.
Street in Murnau. **1909.**
Private Collection.
This work dates from the
period when Kandinsky
took over the *Neue
Künstlervereinigung* (the
New Artists' Union). Some
areas of the painting are
triumphant declarations
of the power of colour. The
contrasts, especially
between the yellows and
blues, give the painting
extraordinary vitality.

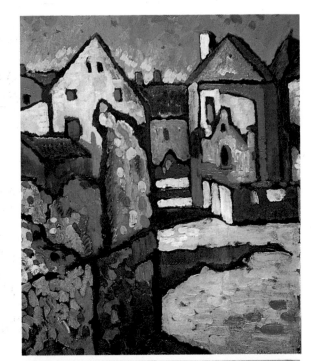

FRANZ MARC. *Blue
Horse 1.* **1911. City
Gallery, Munich.**
Franz Marc loved painting
animals. Horses, especially
blue ones like this example,
appear time and again in
his paintings. Although
normal perspective is
absent from many of his
works, he manages to
achieve a feeling of depth
through his wise choice
of colours.

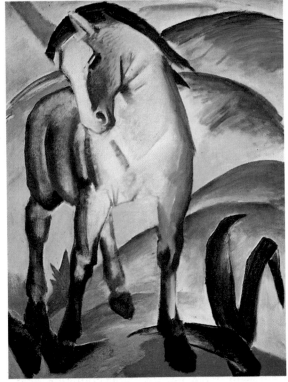

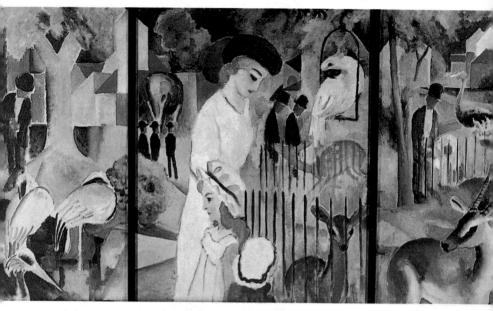

sexual themes, which were previously forbidden, came to be acceptable artistic subjects.

In terms of form, Expressionism was greatly influenced by native African art. The artists frequently returned to a schematic way of representing human figures or landscapes. Like the Fauvists in France, the Expressionists favoured a palette full of vibrant and contrasting colours.

In 1910, the *Die Brücke* artists moved to Berlin, where a publication called *Der Sturm* was being published. Founded and edited by Herwart Walden, this was the first of many publications which sought to spread the Expressionist philosophy. Walden also opened a gallery in which Expressionist works were shown. In addition to exhibiting works of the *Die Brücke* artists, this gallery showed the works of a second Expressionist group called *Der blaue Reiter*.

This second group had formed in Munich toward the end of 1910. Its members included Vasily Kandinsky, Franz Marc, and August Macke. Their main work was the publication of a well-

AUGUST MACKE. *Great Zoological Garden.* **1913. Ostwall Museum, Dortmund.**
The zoo, one of Macke's favourite themes, is treated here as a large triptych, a panel divided into three side-by-side units. Human figures, several species of animals, and areas devoted to lush trees are combined to give dynamic movement to the picture. Colour again reinforces this effect. Macke's compositions are usually very lyrical, using soft colours and soft lines.

GEORG GROSZ. *Fair Spain, Far Away in the South.* **1919. Klaus Hegewisch Collection, Hamburg.**
Bitter criticism of middle class society, its depravity and vices, is a frequent theme of paintings by Grosz. In this watercolour, the lines of the drawing itself mix with bold, vibrant splashes of colour. Music from a gramophone fills the cabaret-like scene. The painting's title, written in German, appears amid the notes.

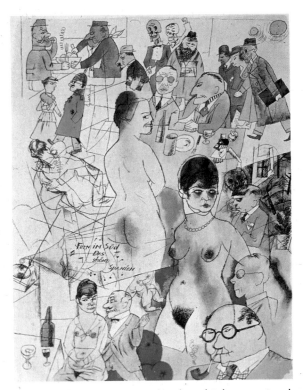

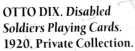

OTTO DIX. *Disabled Soldiers Playing Cards.* **1920. Private Collection.**
A crude criticism of the military establishment is implied in this painting. The little that remains of the three wounded soldiers is shown as they play cards against an Expressionist background.

known almanac or yearbook, which contained the works of a wide range of artists. Kandinsky, who was the core member of *Der blaue Reiter,* favoured the idea of total art, which implies the acceptance of any artistic manifestation, however extraordinary it might appear. Folk art, children's art, and work from the Far East and Africa all appeared on the pages of the almanac. Contributions from European artists outside of Germany were encouraged. The French painter Le Fauconnier informed readers of the latest developments in Cubism, which was the leading style in Paris. The almanac achieved great success and was intended to be published annually. However, because of the war, only one issue was ever published.

The finished works of the *blaue Reiter* group and the Dresden artists differ greatly. Curved lines

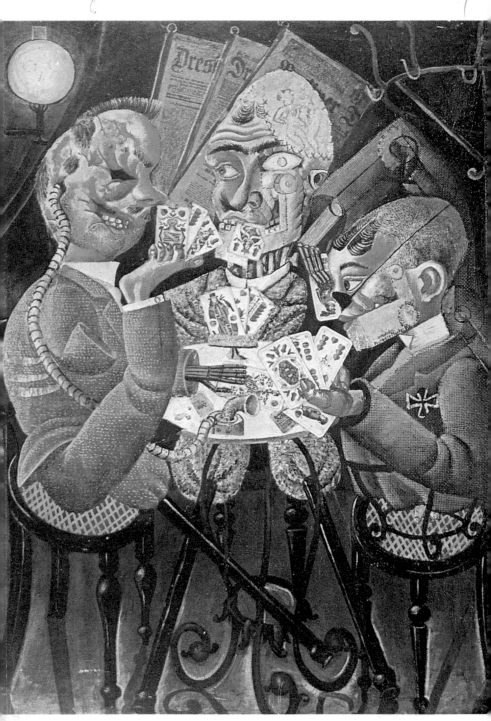

25

prevail in the work of the *blaue Reiter* group as opposed to the zigzag lines favoured by Kirchner and other members of *Die Brücke*. The colours used by the *blaue Reiter* group tend to be softer, and in general, their work tends to be more dreamlike and lyrical.

The careers of many of the artists were cut short

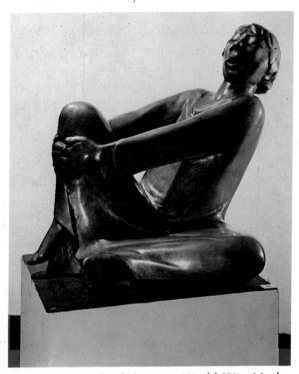

ERNST BARLACH.
Singing Man. **1928.**
Wallraf-Richartz
Museum, Cologne.
The combination of straight and curved lines is one characteristic of Barlach's sculpture. The expressivity of his figures is retained throughout all his work. As well as being a fine sculptor, Barlach also produced a large number of etchings and lithographic plates.

by the outbreak of the First World War. Macke and Marc were killed at the front. Kandinsky left for Russia, where he remained until 1921, when Walter Gropius invited him back to Germany to teach at the Bauhaus School. Few managed to pursue their careers during the war years, so a revival of Expressionist art was not seen until the '20s.

From the 1920s until the rise of the Nazis in 1933, Expressionism coexisted with another concept called *Neue Sachlichkeit* (New Realism or

Objectivity). This is seen as the third phase of Expressionism, following the *Die Brücke* and *Der blaue Reiter* phases. With this new phase, artists were much more aware of their individuality than they were of working as an integrated group. A bitter pessimism pervaded the later Expressionist work, which often depicted poverty or satirized institutions, particularly the army. Another focal point of Expressionism was Vienna, where Oscar Kokoschka worked. Thick paint and curvilinear forms characterized his paintings.

Architecture was an important feature of Expressionist art. Expressionist architecture is indeed attractive because of its richness and diversity.

Perhaps the leading Expressionist form in architecture is the so-called organic style, which aims

OSCAR KOKOSCHKA.
The Tempest (The Wind-Bride). **1914. Museum of Art, Basel.**
In this painting, the artist and his mistress, Alma Mahler, are seen in a close embrace. Though easily ascribed to the German Expressionist school, Kokoschka's work has elements which link it with 17th century Venetian masters. This work dates from the time of Kokoschka's journey to Italy to study the works of those artists whom he admired.

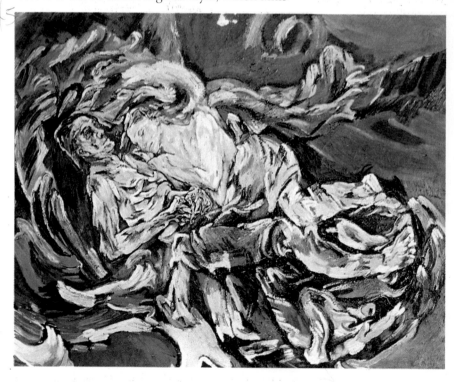

EMIL NOLDE. *The Last Supper*. 1909. Ada and Emil Nolde Foundation, Seebüll.

Many of Nolde's paintings have a religious theme. An interesting characteristic of these works is the non-traditional way in which well-known scenes are represented. Here, for example, the table at which the apostles are usually depicted has been abandoned for a circular grouping around Christ.

to reflect nature. The Einstein Tower in Potsdam, by Erich Mendelsohn, and the Casa Chile by Fritz Höger, are two of the most striking examples of this type of architecture.

Without a doubt, the best known example of Expressionist architecture is the Goetheanum, by Rudolf Steiner, in Dornach, Switzerland. After this building was destroyed by fire in 1914, a second one was built in a similar style, between 1925 and 1928.

Steiner himself was not a trained architect, although he had attended courses at the Vienna High School of Technology. He viewed architecture as a means of expressing nature's rhythmical laws

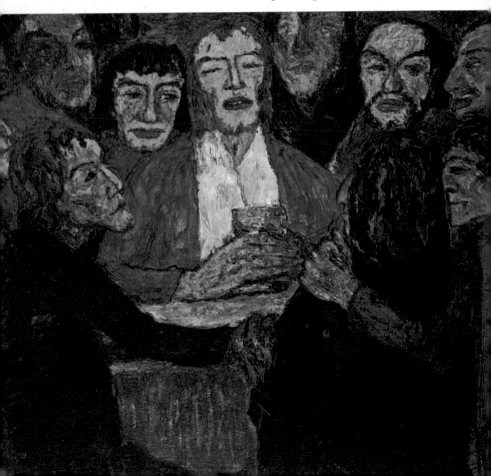

in space. He sought to recreate in his building the forms found in the living world.

In his Dornach building, Steiner pays homage to Goethe, one of Germany's most famous writers. The aesthetic feelings and the elements within the building can be traced to Goethe's ideas. The two domes symbolize the dual face of human nature, and the positioning of the columns represents the different phases of human development. Irregular open spaces and an unpredictable layout of corridors copy the human respiratory system. Colour also plays an important role since, for Goethe, it possessed a spiritual and symbolic character relating to mankind. To fully appreciate the Goetheanum, a visitor must be continually on the move. This is where its novelty and attraction lie. Since Steiner avoided any frontal visualization or the use of symmetry, the Goetheanum could almost be considered a product of one of today's architectural trends.

Expressionism in the Paris School

Though Expressionism is seen as an art form restricted mainly to Germany, artists whose work can be called Expressionist existed in other European countries. The most interesting of these artists belonged to the Paris school.

The French artist Georges Rouault, for instance, avoided Fauvist solutions in his work. He preferred dark colours and heavy lines, which make his figures stand out.

Amedeo Modigliani was born in Italy, but he lived in Paris from the time of his youth. Though he visited the same haunts as Picasso and his Fauvist friends, Modigliani's paintings and sculptures show no common ground with their work.

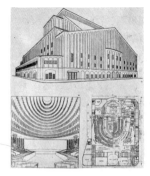

HANS POELZIG. *Grand Theatre*. 1919. Private Collection.
The Grand Theatre complies, both inside and out, with the Expressionist concept of architecture. Curved structures interact with zigzag lines. The vast interior is formed from concentric circles with a stalactite-like decoration.

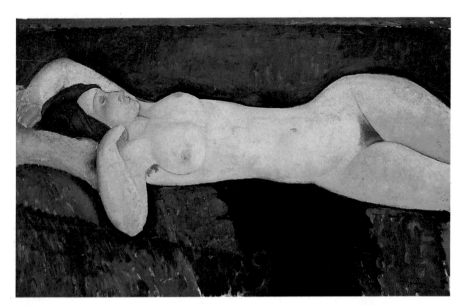

AMEDEO MODIGLIANI.
Large Reclining Nude.
**1918-19. Museum of
Modern Art, New York.**
In Modigliani's series of
reclining nudes, the
influence of the Italian
Renaissance tradition can
be seen, especially that of
Giorgione and Titian.
Modigliani was inspired
not only with their themes,
but also with their com-
position and flesh tones.
Modigliani's painting differs
from theirs mainly in
perspective and the resulting treatment of space.

For some art historians, Modigliani is an odd type
of Expressionist, who was greatly influenced by
primitive art and by his contemporary, Constantin
Brancusi. Apart from portraits, Modigliani painted
a great number of nudes, recalling the Renaissance
tradition of the painted Venus.

Marc Chagall was a Russian artist who settled
in Paris in 1910. Due to the extraordinary individuality of his painting at that time, it would not be
fair to label him as belonging to any particular
style. But there are traces of German Expressionism
in his work, as well as elements of Cubism and
Futurism.

Cubism

The origins of the Cubist movement can be
traced to 1907, the year in which Picasso
painted *Les Demoiselles d'Avignon*. This
painting is a geometric composition that shows
a considerable relationship with Paul Cézanne,

who is considered by some to be a precursor of Cubism. At the bottom of the picture is a distorted fragment of a still life, similar to some painted by Cézanne. Cézanne's death in 1906 and the great exhibition of his work that was organized in Paris the following year played a vital role in the birth of Cubism.

Cézanne's technique shows his great liking for geometric shapes, but his most revolutionary innovation as a painter was in his personal treatment and conception of space. Cézanne abandoned traditional linear perspective, giving colour the priority in creating an impression of space and depth. In his series of paintings dedicated to the

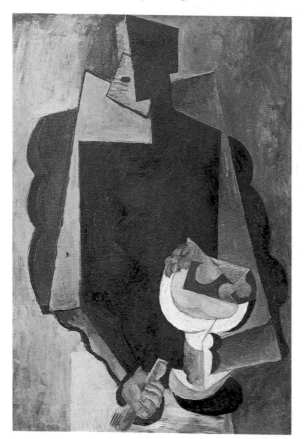

PABLO PICASSO. *Man with Fruit Bowl*. 1917. Picasso Museum, Barcelona.
This is one of Picasso's works in the style known as **Synthetic Cubism.** The figure of a man with superimposed geometric shapes forms the main part of the work. The hand and the bowl are painted realistically and soften the stiffness of the whole composition.

Sainte-Victoire Mountain, Cézanne used ochre, beige, and tan colours in the foreground, with grey and blue tones in the distance. These two colour

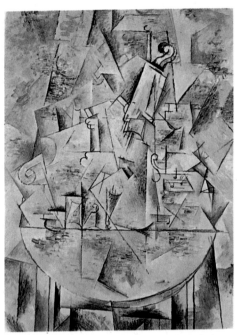

ranges—the first warm and the second cool—were extensively used by early Cubist painters.

Pablo Picasso, Georges Braque, and Juan Gris are considered the orthodox representatives of Cubism. There were, however, many other painters whose works can be labelled Cubist, including Albert Gleizes and Jean Metzinger, authors of the first work on Cubism, entitled *About Cubism.* Other Cubist artists include Fernand Léger, Robert Delaunay, Francis Picabia, Marcel Duchamp, and André Lhote.

Critic and poet Guillaume Apollinaire was the first to formally classify the different types of Cubism that existed in 1913. He published a book that year entitled *Aesthetic Meditations—the Cubist Painters.* This was the work that spread Cubist

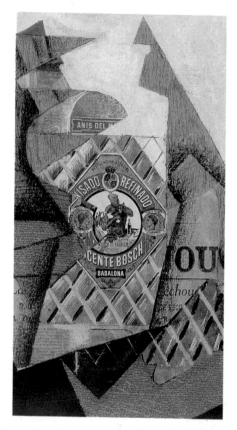

JUAN GRIS. *The Anis Bottle*. **1914. Private Collection.**
This is a typical Gris collage in which he has used pencil over oil and glued paper. In this simple composition, geometric form prevails, but the real world—the label on the bottle—holds centre stage.

theories abroad and enabled this French-born movement to become intermingled with other contemporary European styles.

Art historians recognize two distinct types of Cubism, corresponding to two different periods. The earlier, lasting until 1911, is called Analytical Cubism. After 1912, Synthetic Cubism developed with the introduction of collage.

In Analytical works, the artist mentally breaks up the real world of his subject, then reassembles it using geometric shapes.

Over time, Cubism tended more toward realism. Real objects began to play a larger role in compositions and were sometimes actually glued to the canvas. They were also depicted more faithfully. Collage was, without a doubt, Cubism's greatest

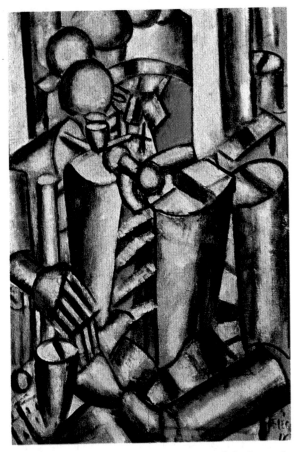

FERNAND LÉGER.
Soldier with Pipe. **1916.**
Private Collection.
Léger had a very personal
approach to Cubism.
Cylindrical shapes appear
everywhere in his work.
The colours that he uses
are also unique. He adds
metallic brilliance to
neutral and primary colours,
which may reflect his love
of machinery.

achievement. It spread rapidly beyond the boundaries of Cubism and was accepted and used by many artists.

The revolution that occurred in painting after the discovery of collage is one of the most remarkable aspects of the artistic scene in the 20th century. Items such as paper, cardboard, fabrics, and netting, stuck directly onto the painting, greatly enriched the compositions. Using these everyday objects as part of the paintings seemed to change the whole idea of art.

Cubist sculptors often chose to use rounded shapes, and worked with all sorts of materials. The bronzes of Raymond Duchamp-Villon seem

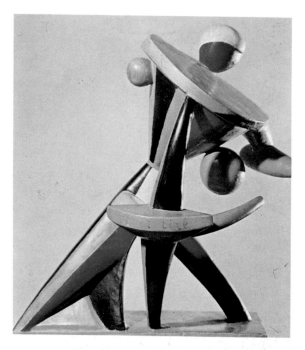

ALEXANDER ARCHIPENKO. *Pierrot.* **1913.**
This sculpture is made of painted wood, and the moving human figure has been broken down into distinct geometric parts. Its sense of disjointedness shows how much Cubist sculptors are indebted to collage.

to exhibit a primitive style. His style differs completely from the complicated structures in painted wood by Alexander Archipenko, whose work is possibly more closely akin to that of the Cubist painters. Jacques Lipchitz was another important Cubist sculptor, whose works in stone are pure Synthetic Cubism, consisting of strictly geometric planes.

Constantin Brancusi is a Romanian sculptor who settled in Paris. His early works in stone, which greatly influenced Modigliani, are certainly allied to Cubism because of their geometric shapes. In later works, however, Brancusi developed his characteristic ovoid, or egg-shaped, works in metal and bronze.

The works of Henri Laurens are also unique. Under the influence of his friendship with Braque, he began a series of three-dimensional works in 1911, which express his own personal understanding of collage. They are assemblages, or

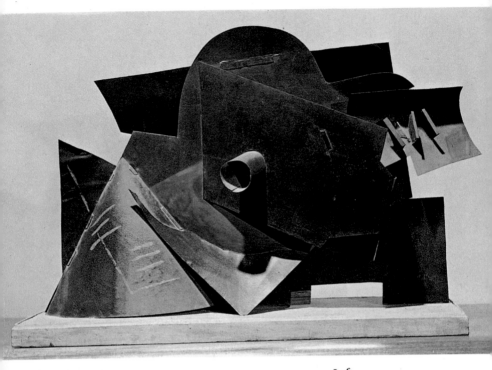

Above,
HENRI LAURENS.
The Guitar. **c.1914.**
Private Collection.

Some parts of this sheet
metal construction by
Laurens are painted in
bright colours. The pieces
are assembled in planes,
using the same technique
as in Cubist paintings. The
idea of using sheet metal
opened up a whole new
range of possibilities, since
sculpture had been
restricted to traditional,
but costly, materials.

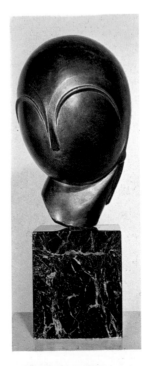

Left,
CONSTANTIN
BRANCUSI. *Miss Pogany.*
1913. Museum of Modern
Art, New York.

Miss Pogany was Brancusi's
model at different periods
of his career, and he made
several distinctive
sculptures with her as the
subject. He used different
materials for these
sculptures, but the ovoid
shape remained a constant
in them all. His use of
smooth, highly polished
surfaces gives an indi-
vidualistic and simple
character to these pieces,
which are difficult to
compare with the work of
any other 20th century
sculptor.

compositions, in wood, which anticipate later Dadaist work. His use of stone and bronze greatly altered the character of his own later works.

The Cubist contribution to 20th century sculpture introduced a fresh way of looking at space. The whole concept of solid, compact space gave way to the idea of articulated space. Slowly an idea was forming which would culminate in the Constructivist works of Naum Gabo and Antoine Pevsner and their conception of aerial sculpture. With their sculpture, the space and air in and around the work is as important as the sculpture itself.

Italian Futurism

Though most of the Futurist artists already knew one another at the turn of the century, the movement itself did not take shape until 1909. That was the year that Filippo Tommaso Marinetti, the group's ideologist, published the first Futurist manifesto. A well-known, if brutal, sentence in the manifesto sums up the Futurist creed: "a motor car, sounding like a machine gun, is more beautiful than the *Winged Victory of Samothrace*." This assertion makes clear the basis of Futurist ideology—their total and absolute rejec-

UMBERTO BOCCIONI. *The City Grows*. 1910. Museum of Modern Art, New York.
The restless energy of the Futurists is even more significant in Boccioni's work, since he seems preoccupied with including their formal ideas in all his paintings. His oil paintings dedicated to the construction of the city are the only exception to this rule. In these, he uses scaffolding and beams to create a vision of a hectic city.

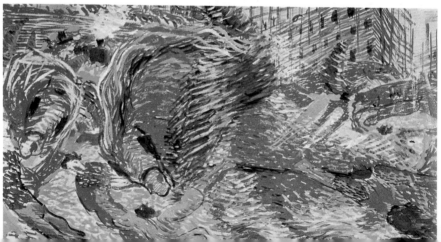

UMBERTO BOCCIONI.
Development of a Bottle in Space. **1912. Museum of Modern Art, New York.**
Boccioni did not leave many works behind, since he died in 1916 when he was in his early 30s. The high quality of his works, however, makes him one of the most representative sculptors, not just of the Futurist movement in Italy, but of the 20th century. Here a bottle is used to experiment with spatial solutions.

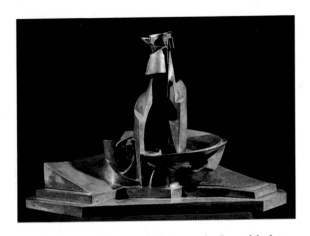

tion of past values and their goal of establishing the merits of the future. Ideas of Modernism are closely linked to this aim of vindication of the future. This is evident in many works by Futurist painters such as Umberto Boccioni, Carlo Carrà, Giacomo Balla, and Gino Severini, who all use the modern world as their subject. The *city* is an endless source of inspiration for Futurist artists. Everywhere, houses are being built, people walk in busy streets, and there are electric lights, restaurants, bars, cars, and bicycles.

Futurist artists, among whom Boccioni is the best known, all used the human figure as a model for their paintings and sculptures. They used a

GIACOMO BALLA.
Hands of a Violinist. **1912. Private Collection.**
Simultaneity makes the representation of movement and the sensation of speed possible by using colour changes to achieve the desired dynamism. Balla was one Futurist painter who came close to abstract art, especially between 1913 and 1914, when his works were limited to geometric shapes and contrasting colours.

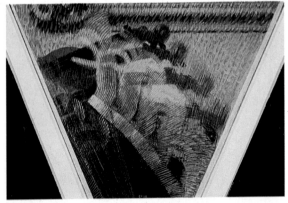

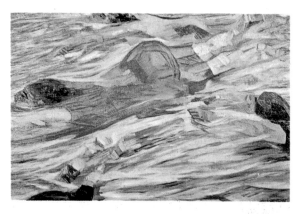

CARLO CARRÀ.
Swimmers. **1910.**
**Carnegie Institute,
Pittsburgh.**
Before he turned to meta-physical art, influenced by Giorgio de Chirico, Carrà's work was very closely allied to Futurist theories. In addition to being able to sense movement, one can almost experience the sensation of speed in this picture.

technique called divisionism to achieve the dynamic effect they all sought so obsessively.

The main goal of Futurist works was to represent movement, change, and transformation,

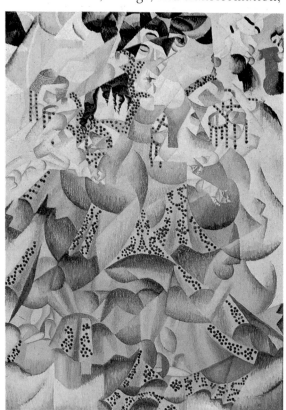

GINO SEVERINI.
Ballerina in Blue. **1912.**
**Gianni Mattioli
Collection, Milan.**
Severini was the only painter in the group who used women as models, frequently as dancers. He used simultaneity and pointillism in his search for dynamic movement. The various tones and intensities of blue are used to create accents.

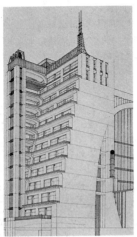

ANTONIO SANT'ELIA.
*Project for a Building
with External Lifts.* **1914.**
In 1914, Sant'Elia presented
drawings for his *Citta Nuova*
at an exhibition organized
by *Nuove Tendenze* in Milan.
The text of the exhibition
catalogue was later used in
the Futurist architectural
manifesto. Sant'Elia's
thoughts seem to agree
with the Futurist ideals,
though he himself was not
a member of the movement.

which were thought to demonstrate progress.

The Futurists were the first to perfect a system to depict the sensation of movement. This system was called **simultaneity.** It was a technique that used the repetition of superimposed images—similar to that of a film sequence—to create the feeling of movement. To achieve a dynamic effect, Futurists used varied, intense, and contrasting colours.

Futurism had connections with Cubism, though geometric form is not itself a Futurist goal. The influence of abstract art on the Italian movement cannot be ignored, as is evident in Boccioni's works entitled *States of Mind*.

Two events shortened the life of the Futurist movement. The first was the premature death of Boccioni, and the second was the new style adopted by Carrà in 1914, when he turned to metaphysical painting.

Futurist architecture is best represented by the projects of Antonio Sant'Elia, whose designs for factories show his preoccupation with applying modernism to buildings.

The style in which the Futurists put forward their ideas in the manifesto was certainly aggressive. The text is full of anti-establishment thought, denunciation of the present state of affairs, and personal attacks on well-known philosophers and literary figures of the 19th century. Futurism was a breeding ground for later movements such as Dadaism and Surrealism.

GIORGIO DE CHIRICO.
Hector and Andromache.
**1917. Gianni Mattioli
Collection, Milan.**
Chirico's work depicts
people as mannequins,
often standing in
mysterious squares of
Renaissance-style build-
ings, which he constructs
using a linear perspective.
These are all elements
which are typically found
in the paintings of this
Italian metaphysical artist.

40

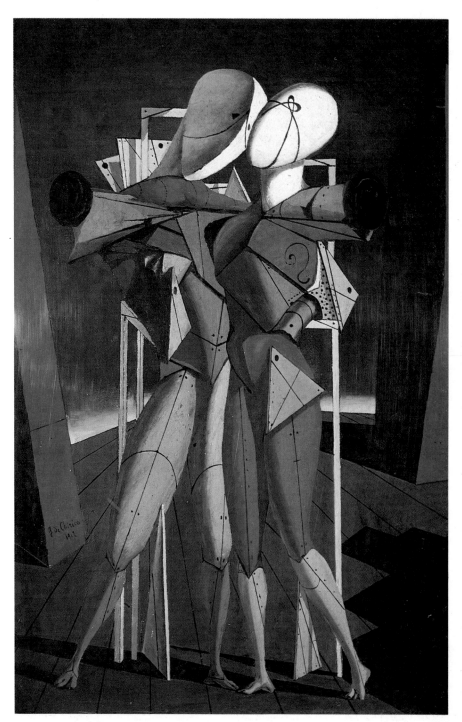

VASILY KANDINSKY.
Painting with a Black Arch. **1912. Pompidou Centre, Paris.**
During the period that he was a member of *Der blaue Reiter* group, Kandinsky's work was both figurative and abstract. Colour is given a full role in all his abstract compositions, as is the notion of rhythm. It is rhythm interacting with colour which results in Kandinsky's sense of liberty.

Abstract Art

Kandinsky gave birth to the abstract movement in 1910, with his first abstract watercolour. His early paintings display a great sense of dynamism and vitality. Colour reigns supreme in these works, in contrast to his later Bauhaus period.

A study of the evolution of Kandinsky's work reveals two distinct periods: one from 1910 to 1921, and another from 1921 until his death in 1944.

During the first period he was fully committed to teaching his theories on art, contained in

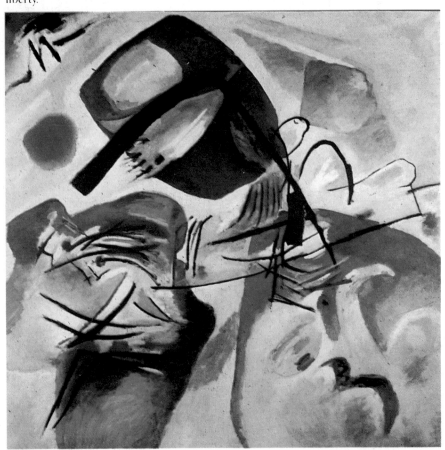

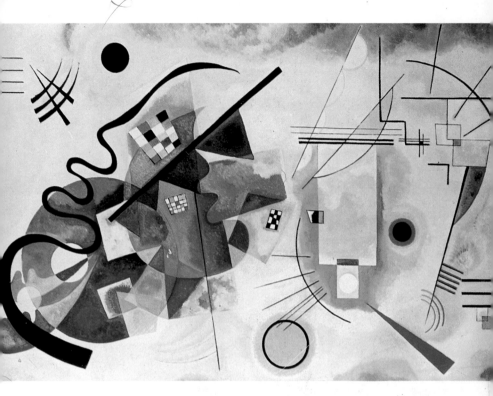

Concerning the Spiritual in Art. The second period revolved around the theories he expounded in a second book, *Point and Line to Plane.* Subjective ideas about the interrelationship between music and painting abound in the first book, resulting in a whole series of extraordinarily creative paintings. When he was teaching at the Bauhaus, however, his writings advocated the triumph of rationalism (the belief that reason in itself is the most superior kind of knowledge). His painting style changed, and he produced many strictly geometric paintings, in which the different elements of colour, size, and line are all very carefully balanced.

Kandinsky's importance lies not only in his works, but in the influence he had on art in the 20th century. Movements or tendencies in art after the Second World War owe much to his theories on abstract art.

VASILY KANDINSKY.
Yellow, Red, Blue. **1925.**
Pompidou Centre, Paris.
During the time he was teaching at the Bauhaus, Kandinsky wrote *Point and Line to Plane,* in which he explains his views on the rationalist state of mind. His pictures from this period clearly reflect his theories and are the best way of understanding them. The basic elements in any composition are point and line. These elements, combined with primary and complementary colours, helped Kandinsky create some of the most varied abstract paintings.

43

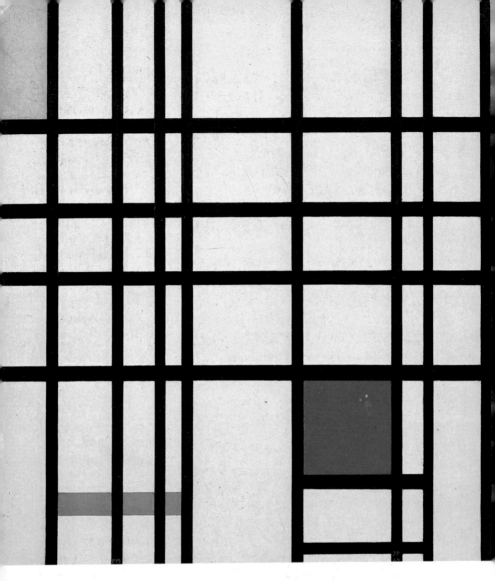

Suprematism is an example of one of the main abstract art styles which played an important role in the 1920s. It was in 1915, after the publication of the Suprematist manifesto that the Russian artist Kasimir Malevich expressed the theories with which he had been experimenting for the previous two years.

In 1909, the first contacts with the avant-garde group had already been made in Russia by Mikhail

Larionov and Natalia Goncharova, who published the Rayonist manifesto. This helped establish the new styles in most Russian cities. It was not difficult, therefore, for Malevich to introduce abstract painting, which was soon to find many followers.

The Dutch movement known as *De Stijl*, which had been started by Piet Mondrian and Theo van Doesburg, shared many of the ideas of Suprematism. Other artists and architects soon joined the movement.

When Theo van Doesburg introduced a new element into his work, the diagonal, Mondrian who was always more restrictive, refused to accept this variation, and their arguments soon adversely affected their work together. Mondrian left the *De Stijl* movement and perfected his own style, which became known as **Neoplasticism.**

Opposite,
PIET MONDRIAN.
Composition in Red,
Yellow and Blue. **1939-41.**
Tate Gallery, London.
Mondrian's strict adherence to the rules of neoplastic composition is reflected in his use of colours and forms. The artist belonged to the *De Stijl* group, and all of his compositions are asymmetric, but still perfectly balanced. He used primary colours plus black and white, and his forms are all rectangular or square.

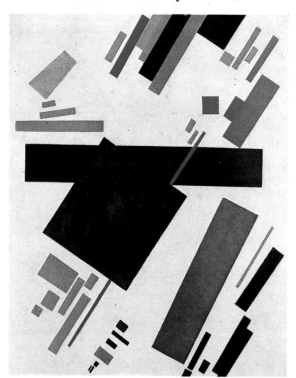

KASIMIR MALEVICH.
Suprematist Painting.
1916. Stedelijk Museum, Amsterdam.
In his first Suprematist paintings, Malevich introduced rectangular and square forms in shallow perspective. These multi-coloured shapes scattered across the white canvas give a dynamic feel to the compositions.

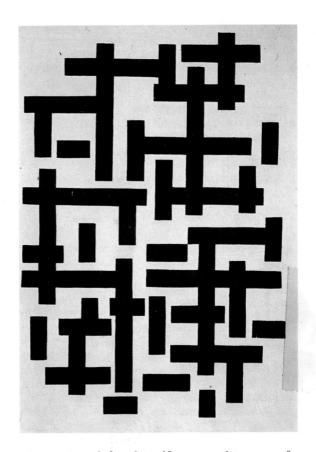

THEO VAN DOESBURG.
Composition in Black and White. **1918. Emmanuel Hoffmann Trust, Basel.**
Black lines of identical thickness form a broken grid on a white background. Geometric abstraction is seen at its best here. This composition is a good example of Neoplasticism, which used black and white, often combined with primary colours, lines, angles, squares, and rectangles.

Rayonism defined itself as a combination of Cubism, Futurism, and a development of Cubism called **Orphism.** It did not offer much that was new, unlike the Suprematism of Malevich. Suprematism affirmed, as Malevich himself declared, the absolute mastery of a pure feeling of form in representational art. His pictures use simple forms and a restricted palette of colours. In many of his works, Malevich took formal simplicity to its extreme, using the canvas itself as the only geometric shape, eliminating colours, and working only in black and white.

Neoplastic theories and ideas soon spread in Holland as well as in Germany, thanks to Bauhaus connections and the *De Stijl* review.

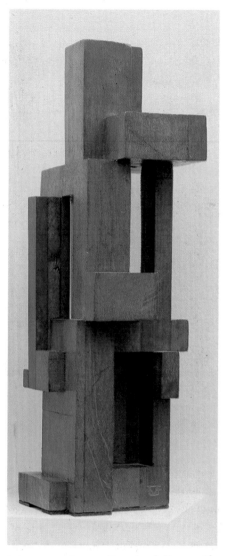

GEORGES VANTONGERLOO. *Construction of Volume Relations.* **1921. Museum of Modern Art, New York.** Parallelograms intertwine in this wooden sculpture by Vantongerloo. The spaces left lighten the whole work. The wood has been smoothed and polished to reveal the grain, and it has been left in its natural colour.

Neoplasticists examine reality carefully, purify and simplify it, and move progressively into abstraction. These artists reject anything that seems superfluous, retaining only the essential. They use regular and right-angled geometric shapes and use primary colours—red, yellow, blue—combined with black and white. Though symmetry is shunned, their works still maintain a sense of balance through the forms and the colours used.

The sculptor Georges Vantongerloo, having first

produced several markedly Cubist works in painted wood, turned to purely abstract sculptures using geometric shapes.

Dadaism

Dadaism brought a completely new approach to the whole concept of art. In their fight against established values, Dadaist artists proposed a complete change, not only in the finished work, but in its very conception.

It seemed appropriate that the Dadaists called their works anti-artistic, since they could not be

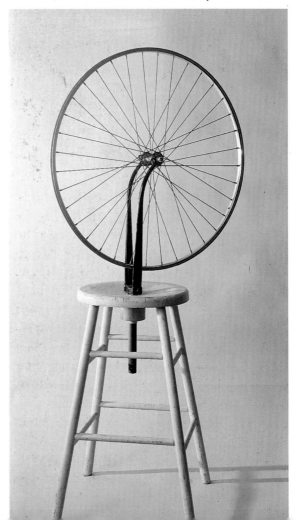

MARCEL DUCHAMP.
Bicycle Wheel. **1913.**
Museum of Modern Art,
New York.
Duchamp's **ready-mades** consist of one or more items taken out of context and reassembled in a totally unexpected way in a new environment. Traditional art critics found it very difficult to attach meaning to these new objects. Duchamp himself described his work as anti-artistic.

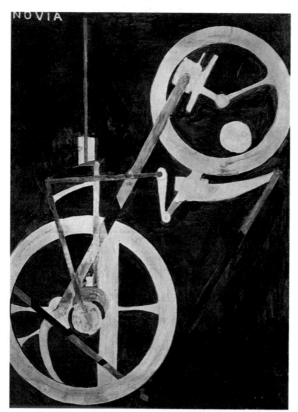

FRANCIS PICABIA.
Bride 1. 1917. **Tzara Collection, Paris.**
This oil painting shows one of the many useless mechanisms so typical of Dadaist philosophy. Gears, wheels, and nuts form a machine which has no useful function. This conveys the Dadaists' ironic reflection on so-called progress and technical inventiveness.

considered works of art by traditional standards.

Dadaism began in Zurich, in 1916, during the First World War. It was closely linked to the opening of the Cabaret Voltaire by the poet Hugo Ball and his girlfriend, Emmy Hennings. There, cultural entertainment such as poetry readings with piano accompaniment, song recitals, and plays was offered to the public. Ball was soon joined by Tristan Tzara, whose fertile imagination produced some superb spectacles. The Janco brothers, from Romania, were also involved with the cabaret from the start.

The shows were soon well known for their aggressiveness and defiance. During the poetry readings, strange sounds were produced by even stranger instruments. Sometimes the artists dis-

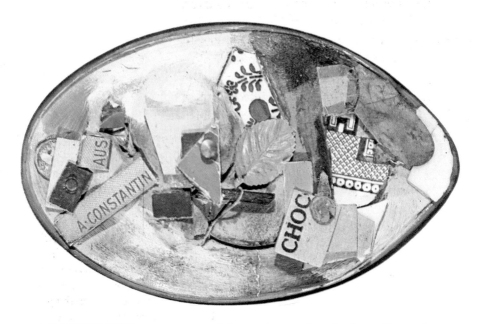

KURT SCHWITTERS.
The Mirror. **1920. Tzara Collection, Paris.**
Schwitters has used a mirror as the background for this collage. It consists of different sorts of paper, broken china, leaves, twigs, and stones blended together in an oil painting. Schwitters' outstanding mastery of the collage technique is seen in his attractive and daring compositions. They range from the abstract to the realistic, but each retains its own freshness and individuality.

guised themselves and rushed into the audience, causing quite an uproar.

Cabaret Voltaire did not last for long in Zurich, but the spirit of Dadaism had been born, and it was not long before Dadaist artists focused on provocation as their main theme. Dadaist work seemed aimless at first, but it was designed to shock the viewer into awareness.

It is difficult to come to terms with Dadaism without any understanding of the personality of its founder, Tristan Tzara. He often maintained that he picked the word *dada* at random from the dictionary. It had no other significance to him. Tzara also said that there never were any governing theories of Dadaism—it was nothing more than a protest.

Dadaism, however, spread rapidly to many cities in Germany, including Berlin, Hanover, and Cologne. In Berlin, Raoul Hausmann and his friend Hannah Höch produced interesting collages and photo-montages.

One very significant member of the Dadaist

movement was Kurt Schwitters, whose collages, such as his well known *Merzbilder,* were the first to incorporate junk objects into their designs. In his Hanover home, he built an extraordinary piece called *Merzbau.* It was constructed of masonry, alternated with cardboard, and painted white. In niches, Schwitters placed small mementos of his artist friends. The whole project grew with time, but it was destroyed during wartime bombing. Only photographs remain of this Dadaist-inspired work.

The rapid spread of Dadaism was due, in part, to the publication of several reviews, such as

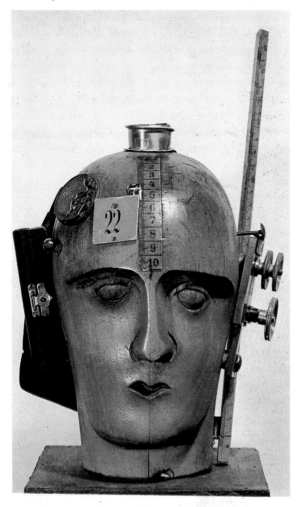

RAOUL HAUSMANN.
Mechanical Head. **1919-20.**
Collection of the artist, Berlin.
This construction clearly shows the aversion the Dadaists had toward machines, as well as their rejection of everything related to machinery. Hausmann has ironically placed a wooden head on instruments to measure the level of intelligence. This is designed to make the viewer reflect upon some of the negative aspects of "progress."

MARCEL DUCHAMP.
The Bride Stripped Bare by Her Bachelors, Even **(also known as *The Large Glass*). 1915-23. Art Museum, Philadelphia.**
This unusual painting is done on glass, using oil, varnish, and melted lead. It is perhaps one of the most daring art works of the 20th century. The imagery of *The Bride* is rather elaborate and has been the subject of much study by art experts. Their interpretations are usually based on the notes that Duchamp published in the famous *Green Box.*

Dada, Die Schammade, and *Camera Work.* The latter, dealing mainly with photo-montage, was published in New York. Many Dadaists had chosen to work in New York, including Man Ray, Francis Picabia, and Marcel Duchamp.

Marcel Duchamp was an authentic forerunner of Dadaism. His ready-mades had stirred up the art world in 1913, as had his *Bicycle Wheel,* poised upside down on a white stool. Other works followed the *Bicycle Wheel,* including *Fountain* (which was a porcelain urinal that Duchamp signed "R. Mutt," the name of a firm of sanitary engineers), *Bottle Rack,* and a work entitled *Why Not Sneeze Rrose Selavy?,* which consisted of an iron cage filled with sugar cubes cut from marble.

Duchamp's major work, however, must be the one entitled *Bride Stripped Bare by Her Bachelors, Even,* which is also known as *The Large Glass.* This work, made between 1915 and 1923, is not a painting, but rather a construction sandwiched between two sheets of glass. Duchamp left a vast number of notes about this work, which were gathered together in the *Green Box,* a collection of his writing, published in 1934. These notes help reveal the meaning of the *Large Glass,* which can seem very obscure at first glance.

Dadaism found many followers in Paris, including several writers. Perhaps the best known of these was André Breton, who became the spiritual leader of the Surrealists a few years later.

There are a number of points in common between Dadaism and the later Surrealism. Many Surrealist artists were first involved with Dadaist art or writing. It would not be fair, however, to pick out only those points which the movements had in common without drawing attention to the fundamental differences between the two styles.

The urge for destruction, which was characteristic of Dadaist work, was never a part of Surrealism. The end of Dadaism was proclaimed

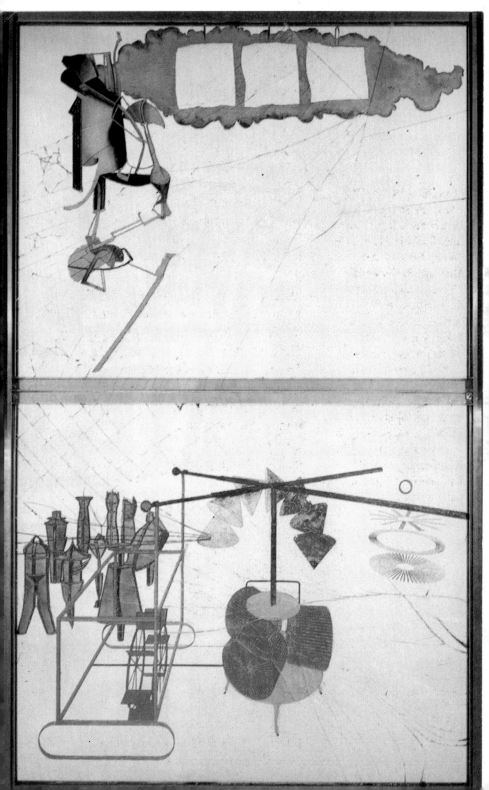

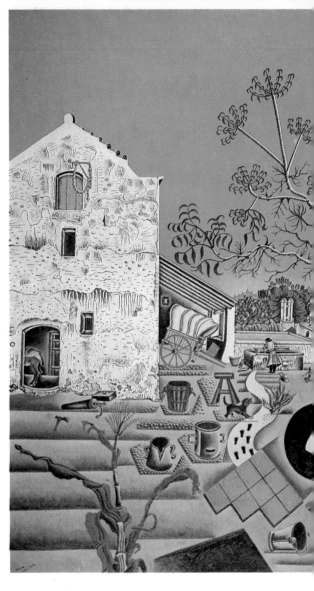

by Tzara himself in 1922, when he pronounced the "Funeral Oration for Dada" in several German cities.

Surrealism

The birth of Surrealism is usually recognized as the day that André Breton published the first Surrealist manifesto in Paris, in 1924. But there are earlier literary works of his which

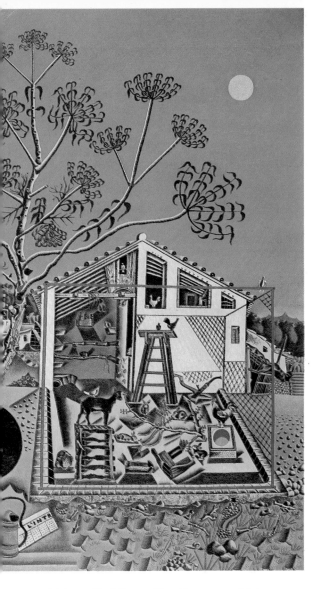

**JOAN MIRÓ. *The Farm.*
1921-22. National Gallery,
Washington.**
The house in Montroig, in
which Miró spent many of
his holidays, has often been
the subject of his paintings.
The meticulous way in
which he portrays tiny
animals is particularly
significant. Tools and farm
equipment, too, are very
accurately represented. *The
Farm* is one of the first
paintings in which Miró
demonstrates his uncanny
ability to portray space in a
balanced manner. Despite
its apparent simplicity, even
naiveté, this picture is very
complex, both in form and
in colour.

could be called Surrealist. Breton and his group
had been followers of Dadaism, and much of their
earlier work can be considered a forerunner of
Surrealism.

Surrealism began as a literary movement, lean-
ing heavily on the personality of Breton, who
quickly became the ideological head of the group.
Breton, a student of psychiatry, had spent his
military service at the Nantes Military Hospital,

working with the mentally ill. He was therefore familiar with psychoanalytical therapy and treatment. He had also studied medicine and was

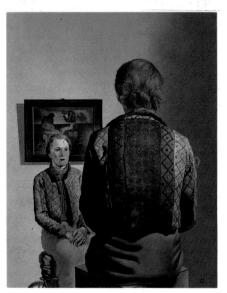

SALVADOR DALI. *Gala and "The Angelus" by Millet*. 1935. Museum of Modern Art, New York. This is one of many of the paintings Dali made in the '30s. It is based upon a painting by Millet with which Dali became obsessed. Behind Gala, Dali's wife, is a version of the painting, but with certain variations. Gala sits facing another figure in the foreground, probably Gala, too—seen from the rear. The two images of Gala reproduce, to some degree, the attitudes of the two figures in Millet's painting.

familiar with Sigmund Freud's work on interpretation of dreams and psychoanalysis, based on the free association of ideas. These experiences formed the basis of his literary work in Surrealism.

Breton's basic concept was one of automatism, a sort of magical direction, coming from the subconscious, which gave rise to poetry, essays, and other writing. Later, painters and sculptors used the same methods in their work.

These surrealist paintings and sculptures fall into two different categories. On the one hand, there are artists who chose pure automatism. On the other, there are those who mix automatism with dream-related experiences. André Masson is one of the leaders of the first group. In 1924, he was already using automatism in some of his pen-and-ink sketches. These were mostly free-style work, showing both dynamism and optimism.

Some of the most interesting of his works are his sand paintings, dating from the second half

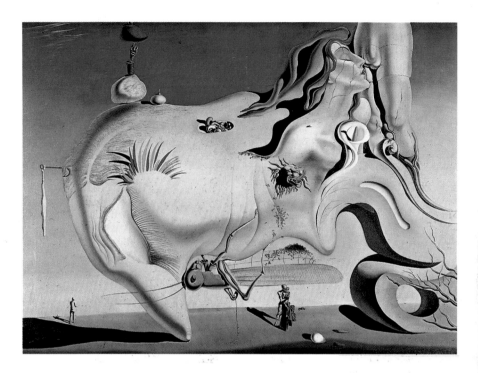

of the 1920s, which set the style for later works. They were completely chance creations. Masson laid the canvas on the floor, covered it with glue, and then sprinkled sand on it. Where the glue was thickest, the sand collected in layers, creating a strong contrast with bare areas of the canvas, which the artist then painted.

Another follower of automatism, though not strongly influenced by it, was Joan Miró. He had settled in Paris the year the manifesto was published and soon contacted the writers and artists who were attracted to Surrealism. But by then he had already developed his own style, and he only incorporated certain Surrealist elements into his paintings. The Surrealist side of Miró is best expressed by some of his extraordinary three-dimensional pieces from the '30s and by some of his symbolically functional creations.

Miró's artistic style was one of signs and of vivid, pure, primary and secondary colours, with some

SALVADOR DALI.
The Great Masturbator.
1929. Private Collection.
Here, Dali's strange imagery is dream-oriented. A whole series of phallic symbols appear with characteristic elements such as the grasshopper clinging near the mouth of a large face resting on its nose. The face is a self-portrait. Ants are seen coming out of the insect's belly. These are seen in many of Dali's paintings.

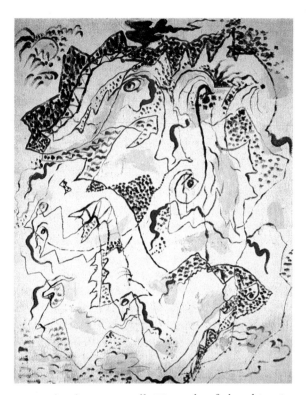

ANDRÉ MASSON. *Horses Attacked by Fish.* **1926. Private Collection.**
Masson painted a series of works depicting battles between sharks and other animals. The idea of cruelty is evoked by streaks of dripping paint suggesting blood.

neutral colours as well. His style of sketching in the human figure and including what he felt to be essential are major recurrent features in his works.

The dream-oriented group is best represented by artists such as René Magritte and Salvador Dali. Both specialized in figurative compositions, following the traditional rules of perspective, and both produced some powerful and significant works.

Magritte chose to combine very different elements in his paintings. Dali, on the other hand, chose double imagery for many of the paintings from his Surrealist period, which spanned approximately 10 years, from 1928 on.

Dali's greatest contribution to Surrealism was, without doubt, his creation of the method which became known as paranoid-critical. This consisted of a free association of the most arbitrary choice of subjects combined with others which appear, almost obsessively, throughout his whole artistic career. For example, *The Angelus* by Millet and *William Tell* appear frequently in his work during the '30s. Dali also worked with the director Luis Buñuel to make what is considered the first Surrealist film, *Un Chien Andalou*. In addition to these works, there is a whole range of symbolically functional objects created by Dali that illustrate his ironic view of the whole Surrealist movement.

Max Ernst's works are also difficult to classify clearly, since they fall between Surrealism and its precursors. The great personal contribution of this German artist, who lived in Paris, is his use of collage in a manner completely different from that of the Cubists. In his collages, Ernst integrates paper in such a way that it becomes impossible to distinguish between collage and the painted surfaces. He also developed the technique known as **frottage.** Frottage means "rubbing," or

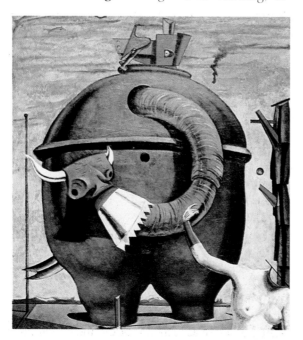

MAX ERNST. *Elephant Celebes.* 1921. Tate Gallery, London. Ernst's work during his Dadaist and Surrealist periods shows no difference in subject or technique. This painting is from the Dadaist era. A large shape, somewhat like an elephant, fills most of the space. The elephant is treated more like a large machine of indeterminate function. An easily recognizable characteristic of Ernst's work is the headless women who appear frequently in his paintings of the '20s.

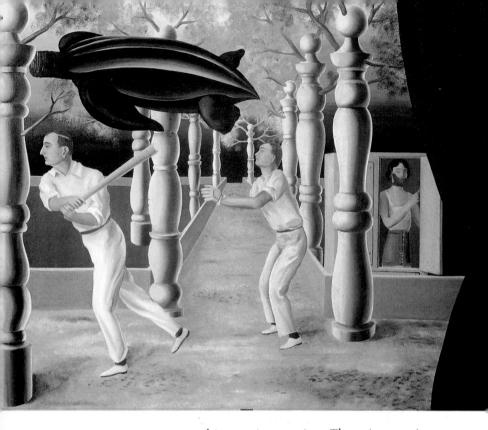

RENÉ MAGRITTE.
The Secret Player. **1927.**
Private Collection.
Magritte is one of the most
representative of the dream-
oriented Surrealist painters.
The most diverse elements
are brought together here, so
that the irrational acquires
special meaning. The attitudes of the figures, as well
as the colours used, are
intended to distance them
from the spectator.

making an impression. These impressions are
then transferred to the canvas. This technique
gives his compositions a great subtlety of texture
and finish which has seldom been equalled.

Jean (Hans) Arp, another Surrealist painter, is
particularly noted for introducing the idea of fate
into his work. Both his paintings and his sculptures of painted wood are abstract, but he does
have a certain taste for some life-like forms. Arp
produced sculptures in metal and stone in the '40s.

Surrealism has the distinction of having spread
across the world. There are two main reasons for
this. André Breton personally spread the Surrealist
word in his many reviews, such as *Surrealism
Serving the Revolution* and *Minotaur.* He also
organized lectures, poetry readings, and exhi-
bitions. In Latin America the movement became
enormously popular in the '40s and remained so

into the '80s. Many European artists, who had maintained contact with the small Surrealist nucleus in Paris, fled to the United States during the Second World War.

It was the revolutionary spirit of Dadaism, kept alive in Surrealism, that spawned the second wave of avant-garde tendencies. The movement called **Abstract Expressionism** produced sculpture and painting with Surrealist characteristics. They are based upon the more daring compositions of some earlier Surrealist artists. Among the best examples of Surrealist sculptures are those of Alberto Giacometti, who lived in Paris and became a member of Breton's group. His pieces from the '20s are strongly linked with primitive art. With the exception of Dali, the Surrealists greatly admired primitive art, and Breton himself had a large collection of masks and carvings from Africa and Oceania.

Giacometti's bronze sculptures, with their longer, finer filaments, attempt to represent human and animal form. His unmistakable style has greatly influenced later generations of sculptors.

Russian Constructivism

Constructivism, led by its founder, Vladimir Tatlin, was at first closely linked to early Russian avant-garde styles, such as Suprematism. In 1920, however, the two groups split because the intentions of the Suprematists differed from those of the Constructivists. Tatlin's ideas for artistic renewal were aimed at motivation of the masses.

Thus, in 1920, Tatlin and his followers proposed the validity of industrial design, as opposed to purely artistic creativity, which they considered a mere offshoot of bourgeois tastes. Constructivists believed that their talent should be dedicated solely to tasks that were useful to society such as archi-

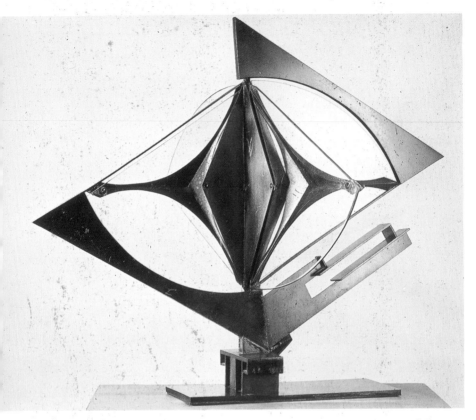

ANTOINE PEVSNER.
Construction. **1923-25.**
Tate Gallery, London.
Pevsner usually chose metal
for his three-dimensional
constructions. Metal sheets
and filaments are used to
create a new concept of
space, far removed from
previous styles. Many of his
works have a marked aero-
dynamic style, which stems
from the perfect marriage
of geometric forms, both
regular and irregular.

tecture, industrial production, commercial design,
and typesetting. Though these objectives might
seem to have much in common, it cannot be
said that Constructivists achieved a style that
could be called united. Perhaps this was because
there was such a diversity among the artists in
the movement.

But Constructivism certainly influenced the
evolution of art and architecture in the 1920s.
Many associations were set up: VCHUTEMAS
(Workshop of Higher Artistic and Technical Design), which was the principal centre for experi-
mentation in Russia; ASNOVA (Association of
New Architects); and the OSA (Society of Contemporary Architects) among others. Constructivist
artists designed most of the political posters of

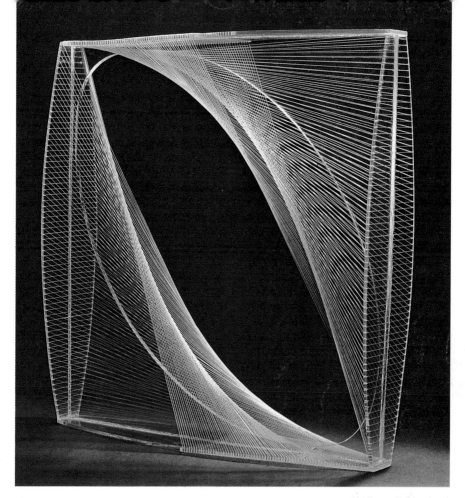

the time, but their really outstanding contribution was in the field of architecture. Tatlin's most famous piece was his project for the *Monument to the Third International,* which he produced in 1919. It can be considered a sculpture or the architectural design it was intended to be. It consists of two sloping, spiralling cylinders, which have much in common with the Italian Futurist movement.

The reawakening of interest in sculpture was due greatly to the two Pevsner brothers, Antoine and Naum, who kept in close touch with what was happening to art in Europe. Naum Pevsner, who later changed his name to Naum Gabo, studied with the *blaue Reiter* group in Munich before

NAUM GABO. *Linear Construction, Variation.* **1942-43. Private Collection.**
Gabo's new ideas on sculpture considered the surrounding space and air as an essential part of the whole work. His use of new materials, such as nylon and plastic, allowed him to achieve this aim. In Gabo's works, the surrounding and enclosed spaces are given equal importance to the structures themselves.

PAUL KLEE. *Villa R*. 1919. Museum of Fine Arts, Basel.

Many of Klee's paintings are landscapes, but none of the others display a large letter of the alphabet as this one does. The huge R somehow gives the whole painting an air of Surrealism, a movement which influenced Klee at about the time this was painted. The general feeling of the painting, however, is more Expressionist than Surrealist.

moving to Paris. His early works date from around 1915 and are constructed from several different materials. Returning to Russia in 1920, he and his brother published a Realist manifesto, which clearly stated the governing principles of their work. They had a preference for abstract form as well as for an equal evaluation of space, time, and light. Based on these ideas, Naum created the first **kinetic sculpture,** in which a small motor causes a thin steel sheet to vibrate, effectively creating a "space."

Antoine Pevsner's career development started somewhat later than that of his brother, but it took a very clear direction after the publication of the manifesto. His work in the '20s cannot be labelled abstract, unlike his later work. Helical (or spiral) constructions, with surfaces made of thin, corroded bronze are his most significant pieces from this period. By far the most important contribution of the two brothers to 20th century art was the aerial conception of their sculptures.

The Bauhaus School

Just a year after the end of the First World War, and in spite of the chaos, misery, and economic plight of Germany, one of the most influential schools of the 20th century was founded. This school, the Bauhaus, was the brainchild of the architect Walter Gropius, who combined the School of Fine Arts with the School of Architecture. It was based in Weimar from 1919 to 1924. Due to financial difficulties, the professors were dismissed and the school had to close in 1924. The second Bauhaus period began a year later, in Dessau, a city with a greater technological heritage than Weimar. There it amply fulfilled its ambitious goals.

Countless functional designs of objects for the

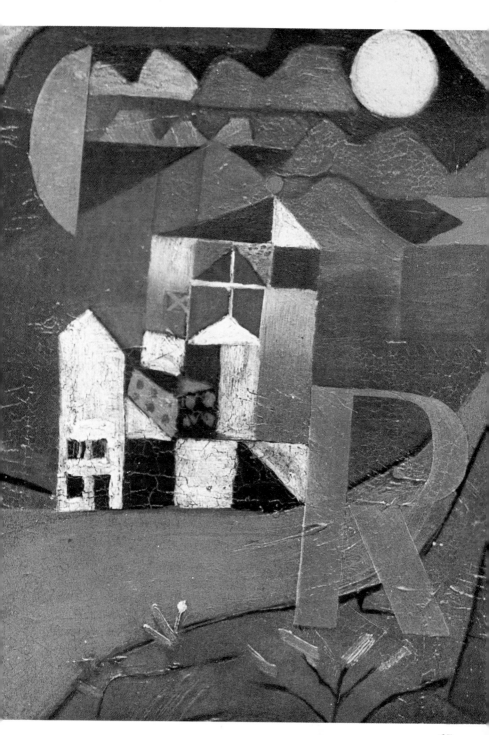

home were produced at the Bauhaus, including wallpaper, upholstery materials, lamps, and furniture. Many of these have been used as models for some of the more revolutionary artifacts of today. This gives a good idea of the importance attached to Bauhaus ideas. It must be remembered, though, that all the professors at the Bauhaus

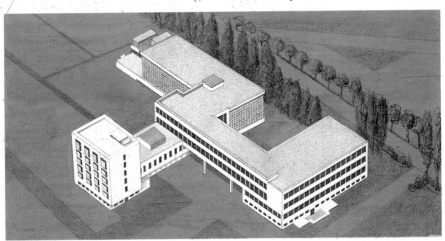

**WALTER GROPIUS.
The Bauhaus Building.
1925-26. Dessau.**

The rational design of this building is clear. Rectangular spaces interrelate, signifying the interplay of the school's disciplines. The building was designed for a number of different functions, but it was essential that an overall sense of unity prevail. Therefore, distinct blocks house the various disciplines, but there is a feeling of voluntary integration imparted by the connecting passages.

were well-known artists in their own right. This gave a great impetus to the creation of a new concept of functionalism. Names like Johannes Itten, Oscar Schlemmer, Vasily Kandinsky, Paul Klee, Laszlo Moholy-Nagy, and Josef Albers represented the high quality achieved at the Bauhaus.

Perhaps the most revolutionary theory expounded at the Bauhaus, apart from its design results, was the way the courses were arranged. Johannes Itten introduced a six-month preliminary course, which was intended to give the student an overall knowledge of all the formalities of any work of art. Proportion, scale, rhythm, light, and shade were studied and discussed. At the same time, experiments were done using different tools and materials. In this way, the student was much better able to choose the workshop in which he or she would study for the next three years.

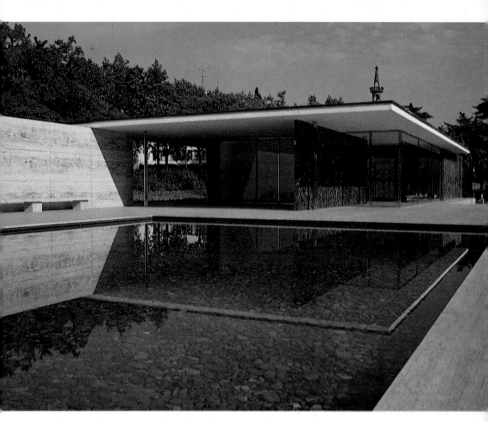

At the Bauhaus, a student had two teachers, a craftsperson/technician and a designer/theoretician. Every workshop submitted designs for objects of everyday use. These projects were hand drawn, but each student also knew how the objects were actually made, since one of the practices was to visit various factories and study the industrial processes. In some cases, selected workers from industry would work alongside teachers at the Bauhaus. After the three-year course, the students took exams to obtain what was known as the "official letter," a proof of the students' knowledge. Once they had this letter, students could continue to study architecture at the Bauhaus in order to obtain a diploma and become a teacher there.

Despite the great work of the Bauhaus, its founder, Gropius, was a constant target of criticism during his time as its leader. Most critics came from ultra-

MIES VAN DER ROHE. German Pavilion for the World Exhibition. 1929. Barcelona.
This pavilion has been reconstructed recently. It is a horizontal structure, with a projecting roof, in typically Functionalist materials—iron, concrete, and glass. Mies van der Rohe's works in Europe all tend to be low, horizontally-oriented buildings, whereas in America he developed his characteristic skyscrapers.

conservative sections of the community, and they forced Gropius to resign in 1928.

His successor was another architect, Hannes Meyer. Meyer directed the school until 1930 and increased the production of the Bauhaus workshops so much that their products became widely known across the world. Between 1930 and 1933, the school was run by Mies van der Rohe, another architect. The Nazis viewed the school as a "nest of Bolsheviks," and it was closed in 1933. In a speech he made in Chicago in 1953 to mark the 70th birthday of Walter Gropius, Mies van der Rohe said that the Bauhaus was nothing more than an idea, which was why it had spread so far across the world and achieved such success. The germ of the Bauhaus idea grew and flourished in the United States, where so many of the artists and architects from the famous school had emigrated after the Second World War. Gropius himself put Bauhaus methods into practice at Harvard University in 1937. Mies van der Rohe introduced Bauhaus concepts when he taught at the Illinois Institute of Technology, in Chicago. Josef Albers developed the Bauhaus preliminary course at Black Mountain College, North Carolina, and Laszlo Moholy-Nagy founded the New Bauhaus in Chicago.

Designers across the world still owe a debt to the Bauhaus. It was the only place (and time) that a personal and individual style was created– a style that was within the framework of rational Functionalism and one that owed everything to the early avant-garde movements.

Functionalism in Architecture

Although the principles were known the century before, Functionalism is the most important of the many architectural styles and trends during the first half of the 20th century.

The concept is based on the premise that "form follows function." Functionalists advocate the idea that interest in architecture stems only from its practicability, and therefore form will always be dependent on function.

Functionalism demands, first of all, that every architectural form should reflect the function for which the building was intended. To this end, building supports, such as beams and pillars, must

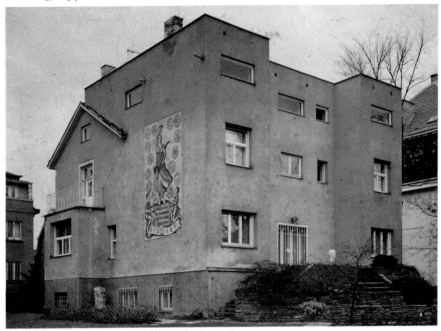

be visible from inside and outside the building.

Second, because Functionalism was a movement closely linked to industrial progress during the first two decades of the 20th century, its technical forms came to resemble machines.

Functionalist architects took many factors into consideration when designing a building, including weather conditions, natural light, and environmental surroundings. The results come close to perfection.

The Functionalist movement is closely linked

ADOLF LOOS. Steiner House. 1910. Vienna.
Loos advocated the abolition of all ornamentation. In his book, *Ornament and Offence*, he refers to the popularity of Modernism, which led architects in Vienna into excesses of ornamentation. Loos called for a total cleanup, which could only be achieved through Rationalism.

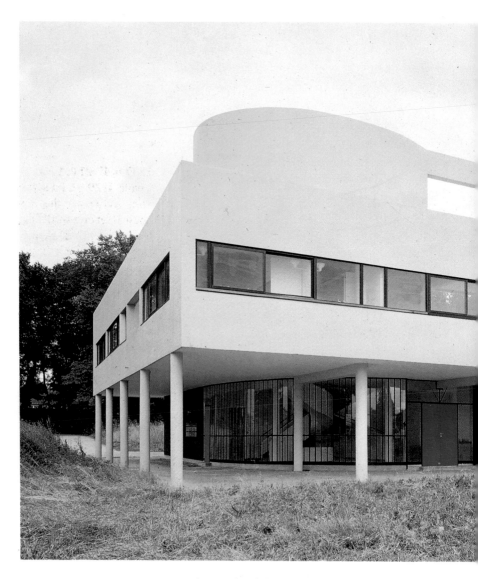

to the work of the Viennese architect Adolf Loos. He rejected Modernism in an attempt to free buildings from excessive decoration.

Loos wrote a book in 1903 called *Ornament and Offence,* denouncing what he saw as the excessive ornamentation, both inside and out, on buildings designed by architects in Austria. His own works are stark examples of the Rationalist

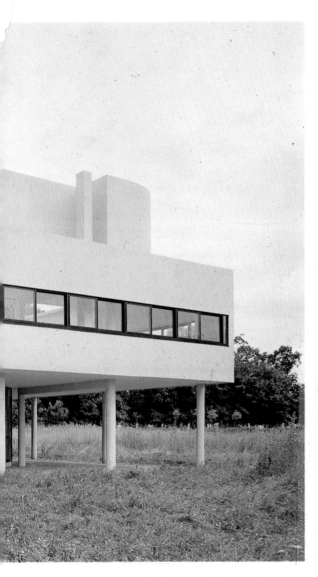

LE CORBUSIER. Villa Savoie. 1929-31. Poissy. Located in France, this house is set on a small hill, with a garden and fields around it. Although there is no main facade, there is a magnificent view from every corner. The solarium on the roof has curving walls, which help deflect the wind.

purity he so stoutly upheld. Two of his best known buildings, the Steiner House and the Tristan Tzara House, show how much architecture around the period of 1910 owed to Loos. He used repetitive cube shapes and concrete painted white. Rectangular doors and windows are the only breaks permitted in the continuity of the facade.

Perhaps the greatest defender of Rationalism

**LE CORBUSIER.
Notre-Dame-du-Haut.
1950-55. Ronchamp.**
This is a view of the east front and external choir of this pilgrimage church in the foothills of the Vosges in France. The most striking element is the concrete roof, which is waterproof and insulating. Sunlight enters through a series of windows, which are placed at different levels and different depths to give changing intensities of illumination at various times of day.

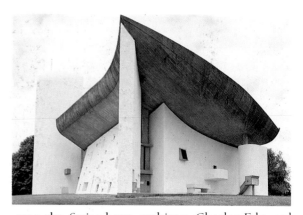

was the Swiss-born architect Charles-Edouard Janneret, known as Le Corbusier. Le Corbusier planned his buildings as machines in which people can live. His aim was to reduce architectural forms to their simplest forms—squares and rectangles for flat surfaces, cubes and cylinders for volume. The interiors of his buildings are designed to fulfill their function. Living space is also divided according to function. The living room may have twice the normal height, or all the rooms may be connected by a single passageway. The house can be enlarged, externally as well as internally, by means of large sliding glass doors. All these principles were applied in his single-family dwelling, Villa Savoie, on the outskirts of Paris.

**LE CORBUSIER.
Unité d'Habitation.
1948-49. Marseilles.**
The basic structure of this apartment block is rectangular. It is made of concrete, on which some rough surfaces have been left as decoration. This is considered the first building in the Brutalist style. Le Corbusier introduced flashes of colour into his design, which contrast sharply with the grey of the concrete.

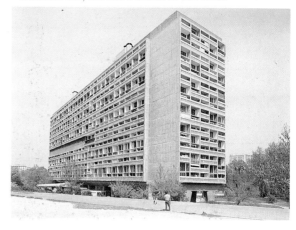

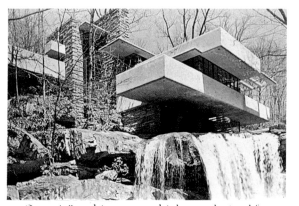

FRANK LLOYD WRIGHT. Kaufmann House, or Falling Water. 1934-36. Bear Run, Pennsylvania.
One of the aims of Wright's work is integration with the environment. Here he uses volume and reinforced concrete, which interact in different projecting roof levels. The whole building resembles the waterfall at its base.

"Organic" architecture, which was derived from Functionalism and shares some common points with it, was a style chosen by Frank Lloyd Wright, another of the great architects of the first half of the 20th century. Wright started studying under Louis Sullivan, part of the Chicago school, which explains the Functionalist similarities in his work. Wright, however, pointed out the danger present in a cold Rationalism devoid of any feeling. He proposed a functional design that he called organic, one which blends the abstract artistic design of the building with the natural elements surrounding it. Wright certainly succeeded in putting this theory to the test in the many family houses he designed.

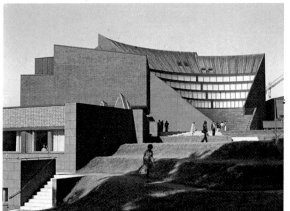

ALVAR AALTO. Polytechnic. Public Concourse. 1949. Otaniemi.
Aalto manages to introduce a touch of regionalism to his Functional architecture by using native materials, such as terra cotta and wood with concrete, iron, and glass.

73

GLOSSARY

abstract art: a style of art that shows the subject in a simplified, often geometric, form; nonrepresentative art

Abstract Expressionism: a 20th-century style of painting that attempts to express feelings and emotions through abstract configurations. These paintings are self-expressive rather than premeditated and show an individuality of form, powerful colour, and almost violent brushwork.

Abstractionism: an artistic style, begun about 1910 by Vasily Kandinsky, which emphasizes the power of colour and design apart from recognizable subject matter

Analytical Cubism: an early Cubist style in which the artist mentally takes apart objects, analyses their various parts, and then rearranges them on canvas in a new way

aerial sculpture: a concept in which the space in and around a sculpture is as important as the work itself

Bauhaus: a German art school, founded in 1919, that stressed science and technology as major resources for art and architecture. Many contemporary designs originated at this school.

Der blaue Reiter: the name of an Expressionist group in Munich led by Vasily Kandinsky

Die Brücke: the name of a group of painters founded in Dresden, Germany, by Ernst Ludwig Kirchner in 1905. The beginning of the German Expressionist movement is attributed to this group.

Constructivism: a Russian art movement, begun about 1910, based on the premise that art should be dedicated only to tasks that are useful to society, such as architecture

collage: a technique in which the artist glues materials, such as paper, cloth, or cardboard, to a background

Cubism: a style of art, begun in 1907, in which the subject is broken apart and reassembled in an abstract form, usually with geometric shapes

Dadaism: an art movement begun in Zurich, Switzerland, in 1916, by Tristan Tzara. It relies on chance and nonsensical elements and is designed to shock the viewer into awareness.

divisionist technique: the painting technique of applying small dots or strokes of colour to a surface so that from a distance they appear to blend together

Fauvism: an early 1900s style of painting opposed to mere copying and one in which there is an absence of any representation of reality. The range of colours used took precedence over the formal composition. Henri Matisse was the leading exponent.

figurative art: a style of art which has representations of form and/or figure

frottage: a technique used by Max Ernst. The term means rubbing or making an impression.

Functionalism: an architectural principle based on the concept that the form a building takes should reflect its function. The concept is based on the premise that "form follows function."

Futurism: an artistic movement, begun about 1909, that rejected past values and promoted the merits of the future

German Expressionism: an art style, begun in Germany before World War I, in which the artist tries to portray strong personal and emotional feeling

Impressionism: an art style, begun in France about 1875, that replaced the traditional concept of representation in painting with a new, simpler, pictoral form based on perception and executed through the interplay of light and colour

kinetic sculpture: sculpture with moving parts

Modernism: a concept that implied innovation and change as well as a rejection of the past

Neoplasticism: an art style that used black and white, often with primary colours, to form geometric shapes

Orphism: a term originated by Guillaume Apollinaire to describe a category of Cubism in which the artist explores the space-creating effects of colour

Post-Impressionism: a term used to indicate various developments in painting in France after the mid-1880s

Rayonism: an art style that combines Cubism, Futurism, and a development of Cubism called Orphism

ready-mades: the term for existing objects placed in an artistic context and presented as works of art. This technique was first used by Marcel Duchamp in 1914.

simultaneity: a system used by Futurists to depict the sensation of movement through the repetition of superimposed images

De Stijl: a Dutch art movement, begun by Piet Mondrian and Theo van Doesburg, that emphasized the use of straight lines and right angles

Suprematism: an abstract art style that emerged during the 1920s. Its theories, set forth by Russian artist Kasimir Malevich, affirm the mastery of form in representational art.

Surrealism: an art and literary movement begun by André Breton in the 1920s. Its basic concepts include automatism (thought coming directly from the subconscious without the intervention of reason) and dream-related experiences.

Synthetic Cubism: the term given to Cubism after 1912 and after the introduction of collage to Cubism

ART THROUGHOUT THE AGES

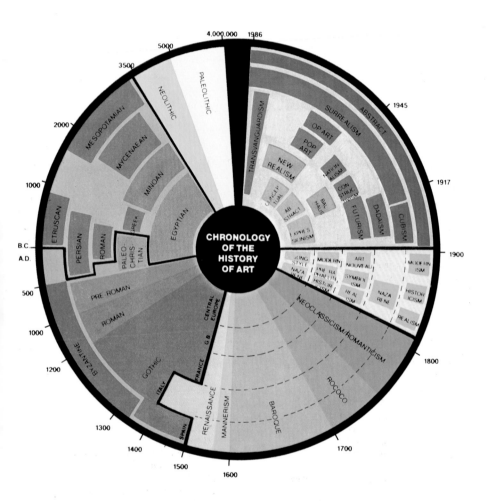

This chart shows the evolution of Western and Near Eastern art through the ages. The terms are those that art historians traditionally use to label periods of time in various cultures where definite stylistic tendencies have occurred. The books in the Key to Art series examine the interplay of artists, ideas, methods, and cultural influences that have affected the evolution of specific art styles.

INDEX OF ILLUSTRATIONS

CONTENTS

FURTHER READING

CHIPP, Herschel, B. (Editor). *Theories of Modern Art.* University of California Press.
HAFTMAN, W. *Painting in the Twentieth Century.* Lund Humphries.
HAMILTON, G. H. *Painting and Sculpture in Europe. 1880–1940.* Pelican History of Art, Penguin Books.
Documents of Twentieth Century Art series. Thames and Hudson.

ACKNOWLEDGMENTS
A.P.: pp. 3, 6, 14, 15, 18, 19, 21, 22 (both), 23, 24, 25, 26, 27, 28, 29, 32, 33, 34, 35, 36 (top), 37, 38 (bottom), 39 (top), 40, 42, 43, 45, 46, 47, 49, 50, 51, 53, 56, 58, 59, 65, 66, 67, 69, 73 (both); Bridgeman-Index: p. 60; Index: pp. 16-17; J. Martin: pp. 30, 44, 48; Oronoz: pp. 5, 9, 20, 31, 36 (bottom), 38 (top), 41, 54-55, 57, 62, 63, 70-71; Scala: pp. 13, 39 (bottom); Sheridan-Index: p. 72 (both).